GOD STORIES

Answered Prayers and Instant Miracles

RON COBY

WESTBOW
PRESS®
A DIVISION OF THOMAS NELSON
& ZONDERVAN

WestBow Press books may be ordered through booksellers or by contacting:

WestBow Press
A Division of Thomas Nelson & Zondervan
1663 Liberty Drive
Bloomington, IN 47403
www.westbowpress.com
844-714-3454

Scripture taken from the King James Version of the Bible.

Scripture taken from the Amplified Bible, Copyright © 1954, 1958, 1962,
1964, 1965, 1987 by The Lockman Foundation. Used with permission.

ISBN: 978-1-6642-3828-2 (sc)
ISBN: 978-1-6642-3827-5 (hc)
ISBN: 978-1-6642-3829-9 (e)

Library of Congress Control Number: 2021912801

Print information available on the last page.

WestBow Press rev. date: 07/30/2021

This book is dedicated to
my Lord and Savior Jesus Christ.

I would like to thank Joni Patterson for her
endless love, her never-ending support, and
for her kindness in giving me the Joyce Meyer
Everyday Life Bible. I'd like to also thank Joyce
Meyer for her inspirational commentary and keen
insights on Scripture in the Everyday Life Bible.

CONTENTS

PREFACE

When God spoke to my heart to write *God Stories*, I set out on a bold mission: Put my faith to the test by proving God, with His Son Jesus Christ, can communicate with His people through answered prayers and created miracles, even instant miracles. This was quite an outrageous goal, and, on the surface, it may sound absurd. However, the contents of this book are filled with incredible stories about God displaying his awesome power in the present moment.

I've had many incredible miracles manifest in my life, yet I had no idea how to accomplish my new mission. However, I knew deep down inside that God would deliver. As I made this miracle request in my prayers, I showed God how much I believed in His power to perform new miracles in my life. I made this decision because I had already experienced so many supernatural events even before writing this book. In my mind, it was a logical decision to make, and one I should have made long ago.

For believers in Jesus Christ, the powerful supernatural experiences you're about to read will either blow your mind, or you'll simply relate to them because you've already encountered many of your own God stories. For nonbelievers, you will either be amazed by these unexplainable happenings because they will be foreign to you, or you will simply pass me off for being delusional. In either case, I hope these spectacular real-life supernatural events speak to your heart, mind, and soul.

Let me tell you up front that I am writing this book with the hope that nonbelievers will find Jesus in their hearts, and believers will head on a new path toward a deeper relationship with God. My deepest desire is that these divinely inspired events, filled with supernatural miracles, will start you on an exciting spiritual journey with God. In addition, after reading this book, I would feel blessed if you would share some of your life-changing God stories with me at rcoby123@gmail.com.

Since I'm writing to those of you searching for God or desiring to experience the present power of Jesus Christ, maybe we can relate with each other? First, I'm certainly not a religious person, but I am deeply spiritual. Next, like many of you reading this book, I don't regularly attend church. Finally, I'm turned off by religious zealots who come off as arrogant, judgmental, and self-righteous.

After reading these spectacular stories, you will see that God is not concerned with your religious acts but with what you believe deep within your heart. In other words, if God can work so dramatically in the life of a flawed person like myself, He can certainly work in your life as well. However, to truly experience the manifestations of God's power in the present moment, certain requirements need to be met. I share all of that with you in this book.

As you read, please stay patient as I go slowly at first but gradually pick up the intensity as chapters progress. My goal is to ease you into these powerful events by going from the semi ordinary to the extraordinary, and finally to the truly unexplainable. I promise you that if you make it to the end of this book, at the very minimum, you will have been highly entertained. However, the upside of finishing this book could change your perspective and greatly enhance your spiritual life. Grab a comfortable chair, put on some relaxing music, and read about the amazing signs, unbelievable miracles, and the incredible visions that I was so blessed to have received from God.

CHAPTER ONE

Jesus Listens

What things soever ye desire, when ye pray, believe
ye receive them, and ye shall have them.

—**Mark 11:24 KJV**

In my first job out of college in 1987, I worked as a margin clerk for
a large brokerage firm on Wall Street. I was miserable because it was
a stressful job filled with one crisis upon another. To make matters
worse, I lived in a rough part of the Bronx where I commuted one
hour each way on a jam-packed subway to New York City. To top it
all off, most of the people I worked for were not very friendly, and
corporate politics led to employees backstabbing one another left and
right. I desperately wanted out of that horrible job, and as someone
who grew up in a small town, I wanted out of the big city.

There was an old Catholic church right across the street from
where I worked. Each morning on my break, I walked over to the
church to pray. I sensed holiness and Christian history upon entering
the Catholic church filled with its paintings of prophets, apostles, and
angels. I would sit down in the pew and look up at Jesus hanging on
His cross. After looking at Jesus and feeling inspired by His powerful
presence, I would get on my knees and pray: *Lord, thank you for dying*

for my sins and for all my wonderful blessings. I ask that you please get me out of this unhappy job and New York City, as I don't belong here. I will look for any door you open, and I will walk through it. Amen.

Jesus Listens to Persistent Prayers

This went on for several months until one day it happened. The CEO of one of the clients I represented at my job was coming to town. He invited me to see a presentation his company was doing for an initial public offering. Afterward, we met outside the venue where he thanked me for what I had done for his brokerage firm. I helped save his company a fortune during the infamous 1987 stock market crash, and he knew it.

Lo and behold, he said, "Ron, I'm very grateful for your diligent efforts on behalf of my firm after the market crashed. Tell me anything, within reason, that I can do for you, and if I can, I'll do it."

I immediately knew this was my door of opportunity—my answered prayer. I responded, "I would like to go work for your firm and become a stockbroker."

He replied, "You want to leave this great city and work for my little brokerage firm in Portland, Oregon?"

I responded, "Yes!"

He said, "You're hired. Is there anything else?"

I answered, "Will you also hire my best friend, Paul?"

He said, "Consider it done."

The entire course of my life changed because of the multiple prayers in that old Catholic church. I moved to Oregon and stayed for the better part of thirty years working in the financial industry. I know without a shadow of a doubt that my consistent prayers resulted in them being answered by God. Also, because I intensely believed, my eyes were wide open for the opportunity once the Lord presented it.

In summary, once Jesus fulfilled His promise and opened the

door for me, I fulfilled mine and walked through it. This was my first lesson in biblical teaching: ask, believe, and receive. As Jesus promised, "What things soever ye desire, when ye pray, believe ye receive them, and ye shall have them." Jesus will listen, but you must believe with all your heart that your prayer will be answered, and then wait expectantly to receive some version of what you asked for in prayer. He will listen, and He will answer in a way that God sees best for your life.

God Will Use His People

And the King will answer them, "Truly, I say to you, as you did it to one of the least of these my brothers, you did it to me." (Matthew 25:40 ESV)

Back in 1989 I took a sales course created by Brian Tracy called the Phoenix Seminar. The man who taught Brian's course was a local stockbroker named Wally. Even though he worked at a competing firm, he was gracious enough to teach Brian's sales course to our company. The Phoenix Seminar literally changed my life. I went from rags to riches in a very short time. Surprisingly, I also received some spiritual riches too.

One early evening after finishing the last sales session for the day, Wally and I were hanging outside my office building together. We were having a pleasant talk about the day's lessons. Suddenly, this homeless man with a shopping cart walked by us. I greeted him, and he responded, "Happy holidays." I felt something powerful radiating from this man, and it created an idea in my mind. I asked him to wait around for five minutes as I had something to give him. With an expectant smile on his face, he agreed.

I went back inside to our company's lunchroom where there was a vending machine for employees to buy soda pop. There was also a gigantic cardboard box about eight feet high and four feet wide where employees tossed their soda cans as they left the lunchroom. I found two super-sized garbage bags and filled them up with pop cans, which are worth five cents each upon return.

I went outside and placed the bags of cans on top of his grocery cart and said, "Merry Christmas!" With a sweet smile on his face and tears in his eyes, the homeless man yelled up to the sky, "Halleluiah, praise the Lord!" He then looked at me and said, "I was just down by the river praying to Jesus for a Christmas present." As he walked away praising the Lord, Wally and I were in awe of what happened. We both knew that the Lord had used me as an instrument to meet that man's prayer. It was a night that I will never forget.

Jesus Teaches

"But when the Son of Man comes in His glory and majesty and all the angels with Him, then He will sit on the throne of His glory. All the nations will be gathered before Him [for judgment]; and He will separate them from one another, as a shepherd separates his sheep from the goats; and He will put the sheep on His right [the place of honor], and the goats on His left [the place of rejection].

"Then the King will say to those on His right, 'Come, you blessed of My Father [you favored of God, appointed to eternal salvation], inherit the kingdom prepared for you from the foundation of the world. For I was hungry, and you gave Me something to eat; I was thirsty, and you gave Me *something* to drink; I was a stranger, and you invited Me in; I was naked, and you clothed Me; I was sick, and you visited Me [with help and ministering care]; I was in prison, and you came to Me [ignoring personal danger].' [37] Then the righteous will answer Him, 'Lord, when did we see You hungry, and feed You, or thirsty, and give You something to drink? And when did we see You as a stranger, and invite You in, or naked, and clothe You? And when did we see You sick, or in prison, and come to You?' The King will answer and say to them, 'I assure you and most solemnly say to you, to the extent that you did it for one of these brothers of Mine, even the least of them, you did it for Me.'" (Matthew 25:31–40 AMP)

Back in 1990 I was a stockbroker working on straight commissions, and I started each month off at zero income. One month, I had all my eggs in one basket, meaning my whole month of commissions was dependent on one big transaction I was diligently working on to close. There was a gentleman named Bill who had worked for a local, publicly traded steel company. Over the years he had acquired a substantial amount of the company's stock, which erupted in price and made Bill a multimillionaire. Once the stock hit his target price, he wanted to sell it on the open market using me as his stockbroker. The plan was to invest the proceeds from the sale into some income–producing products. This had the makings of a nice payday for him and big commissions for me as his stockbroker.

I was a fairly disciplined person when it came to getting up early and being at the office when the stock market opened. However, one morning I overslept, and when I got to my office, I noticed Bill's stock had already hit his selling price. When I listened to my voice messages, a couple of them were from Bill. He had called me to sell his stock. Since I was not at the office, he sold the stock at a competing brokerage house. I was incredibly disappointed in myself for oversleeping because I had just missed a huge payday.

I went for a walk at Portland's Waterfront Park. I sat down on a park bench feeling sorry for myself when somebody sat next to me. I kept my head down in a sulking fashion and acted as if he wasn't there. Suddenly, I heard, "Sure looks like you're having a bad day." I responded, "Yes, it's been a horrible morning." Then I looked at the gentleman next to me. He was wearing secondhand clothing and had an old toolbox on his lap. I also noticed he was in distress. I said to him, "How is your day going?"

He said, "Terrible. I'm a handyman looking for work, but no one will hire me."

I replied, "I'm sorry to hear that."

I then asked him what he was going to do. He said, "Today was my last interview and any remaining hope for a job. I have a wife and kids but no money for food or rent. I'm in a bad situation, and I have nowhere to turn."

I didn't know what to say except, "Have you turned to God and asked Him for help?" And that question set him off in a loud voice.

"Don't preach to me about any of that God stuff! He has done nothing good for me!"

I replied, "He can't help you unless you ask." Once again, he got defensive.

I decided to take a different approach because I sincerely cared about this poor man's troubles. I asked him his name, and he told me it was Pepe. "Pepe, why don't you come back to my office, as I believe I can help you." He agreed. I shut the door and closed the blinds for privacy. "Pepe, I'm on the board of an organization called Union Gospel Missions, and they help homeless families. They can get your family shelter and place you in a job. Would it be okay if we called Don, the man who runs the shelter?" He agreed.

I got the director of the Christian ministry on the phone; "Don, I have a new friend who has been looking for a job with no luck. He might need some shelter soon for his wife and children, but he most certainly needs a job. He's a handyman. Can you find my friend Pepe some work?" He said, "Absolutely, Ron!" I had Don on the speaker phone when he said, "Pepe, don't worry. We have food and shelter for you and your family plus I can get you started with a job right away. Stop by the shelter tomorrow and ask for Don."

After I hung up the phone, I could see Pepe was moved by my efforts to help him. I reached under my desk and grabbed a bunch of *Guidepost* magazine pamphlets. *Guidepost* is a Christian-based magazine that was started by the late Norman Vincent Peale. I grabbed about ten pamphlets and went through each one quickly with him. I said, "Pepe, God loves you, and He wants to help even if you don't want him right now. Norman is an amazing minister, and he has a plain way of speaking about Jesus that you might enjoy.

These are my gifts to you." I could tell Pepe's emotions were stirred. Pepe thanked me and left my office with the *Guidepost* pamphlets and one of my business cards in hand.

The Phone Rang

Lo and behold, about five minutes later, the phone rang, and it was Pepe. He said, "Ron, I'm right around the corner at a telephone booth. I'm calling because I want to tell you something. This morning I was down at that park planning to kill myself as I saw no way out of my troubles. Your kindness today showed me that maybe there is a God. I prayed to him when I left your office." He choked up and finally said, "I'm calling to tell you that everything is going to be okay. God is going to help get me out of this mess. Thank you for the pamphlets and for being so kind to me."

After hanging up the phone, I thanked Jesus for putting Pepe and I together. As I prayed, I was overwhelmed with joy and powerfully filled with the Holy Spirit to the point of such intensity that tears poured down my cheeks. At that exact moment, I understood that Jesus had just taught me the life lesson he preached to his disciples— It is more blessed to give than to receive:

> In everything I have pointed out to you [by example]
> that, by working diligently in this manner, we ought
> to assist the weak, being mindful of the words of the
> Lord Jesus, how He Himself said, it is more blessed
> to give than to receive. (Acts 20:35 AMP)

In summary, this was one of the most impactful experiences of my entire life. The undeniable presence of the Holy Spirit covering my entire being simply cannot be described in words. The blessing and the teaching that I received from the Lord was worth a million times what I could have made in commissions that day. In fact, the experience was priceless. I believe the Lord had me wake up late that morning because He had an important lesson to teach me: It is more blessed to give than to receive.

When I told this story to my pastor, Kip Jacob, he said, "Ron, you may never hear from Pepe again." Kip also said that Jesus used me as his instrument to help Pepe while also teaching me a life lesson and rewarding us both in the process. Kip was right. I never heard from Pepe again, and Jesus touched both our hearts in a powerful way on that miraculous day. Interacting with me on that glorious day may have saved Pepe's life on earth but finding Jesus gave Pepe the promise of eternal life.

> For God so loved the world, that he gave his only begotten Son, that whosoever believeth in him should not perish, but have everlasting life. (John 3:16 KJV)

CHAPTER TWO

Jesus Answers

Call unto me, and I will answer thee, and show thee
great and mighty things, which thou knowest not.

—Jeremiah 33:3 KJV

It was a beautiful Saturday morning in Bend, Oregon, where my son, Joe, and my daughter, Anna, and I were snowboarding on Mount Bachelor. It was a perfect day as the sun glistened off the snow and sparkled in the pine trees. It was a day that I felt wonderfully blessed to be alive, especially because I was doing something fun with two of my children.

I took my children off the main ski hill to the middle of the woods on a semi-groomed trail. This path was not visited often by snowboarders even though it wasn't an extremely difficult side trail to take. My kids followed me down the mountain path, and as we started accelerating, I noticed the trail was both icy and choppy. Sadly, once we started down the narrow path, there was no turning back. Knowing that I had just made a huge mistake, all I could think about was my two kids behind me. Before I knew it, I caught an edge and went flying in the air headfirst into a pine tree.

As I hurled off in midair, I instinctively leaned my head down and went shoulder first into the tree. The collision was bad as I sat under the tree stunned from the crash. Fortunately, my kids were able to safely come to my side. I was completely motionless as Anna asked me, "Dad, are you all right?" I said, "No honey, I'm not. I can't move my arm or shoulder. In fact, I can't move at all. I think I broke something, and I'm in horrible pain. You and Joe need to walk across to the main ski hill and snowboard down the mountain to get the ski patrol to help me. Look around before you go so you will remember where I'm located." Off they went as I lay helpless on the ground with nobody in sight.

Jesus Heals

As I lay hunched over in excruciating pain under the tree, I couldn't believe how badly I was hurting. I recalled the pain felt different from the time when I broke my arm playing soccer as a young boy. I remembered how my broken arm felt totally numb whereas my snowboarding accident left me feeling an intense amount of constant and never-ending pain. Without hesitating any longer, I desperately cried out to God, "Lord, I'm in so much pain that I'm about to pass out. I'm asking You to please help me, as I cannot take this pain much longer."

Lo and behold, the moment my prayer ended, something amazing took place. As I sat motionless in the icy snow, I felt this loving presence surrounding me. Then, without any effort on my part, I felt my arm being lifted, and all of this was happening in slow motion. I found myself in a very peaceful state as this was taking place. The motion in my arm felt like two hands, with the softest touch, were aligning my shoulder. My pain was immediately released as my shoulder popped back into place. This gentle touch of divine power moved my upper arm back into perfect alignment.

This entire spiritual experience that included the surgical-like placement of my shoulder all happened in very slow motion. Once my arm was perfectly and lovingly put back into its proper place, I experienced instant relief from my debilitating pain. In the exact second of my relief, I shouted; "Thank You Jesus!" and at that very moment, the Holy Spirit covered my body, which further confirmed that my cry for help had been answered by God.

Before I was healed, I couldn't move. After the miracle, I was able to get up off the snow and get onto my snowboard, and ski comfortably to the bottom of the mountain. I found Anna and Joe speaking with the ski patrol, and I yelled over to them that I was okay. We all jumped into my car, and I drove home safely where I took some aspirins for pain relief. The next day, I made a visit to an orthopedic surgeon. I told him exactly what had happened, and he said, "Ron, you dislocated your shoulder. I can't explain your spiritual experience except to say that your arm snapped back into its socket, which relieved your pain. You have some tissue damage, but we can get you additional relief with medication and rehab."

In summary, there is absolutely no doubt in my mind as to what happened that day lying on the freezing cold snow under the tree. I experienced a powerful supernatural experience where God instantly answered my cry for help and relieved my pain. The adjustment to my arm and shoulder happened with no effort on my part. It's impossible for me to accurately explain the loving touch that healed me on that day, but there's no doubt that when I cried out to Jesus in pain, he showed me "great and mighty things" with both His holy presence and His loving touch that healed me.

Jesus Is Wisdom

He shall call on me, and I will answer him; I will be with him in trouble, I will deliver him and honor him. (Psalm 91:15 NIV)

One Saturday morning in 2001, I was in distress because I had written a six-figure check to take over my troubled business partnership. Sadly, this action was followed by the local bank unexpectedly calling in a $50,000 business loan. On top of that, the 9-11 terrorist attacks smashed the stocks in my hedge fund. Top it all off with the fact that I had employees to pay and three kids to feed with little money left in the bank.

I decided to go to my office to think about what I was going to do to save myself and be able to feed my family. I quickly realized that only the Lord himself could save me. I was standing when I prayed, *Jesus, I thank You for all the wonderful blessings in my life. I'm in distress, and I don't know what I can do here to survive. Please help me and direct me.*

Lo and behold, I felt something like a bolt of lightning strike directly into my brain. In fact, it was so impactful that it literally knocked me back into my chair. I was in a spiritual trance of some sort when my hand picked up a pen and wrote the following words: **Love Me. Trust Me. The Truth will set you free. The answers are within you now.**

I decided to take those words to heart and apply them in a way where I could improve my dire situation. After deciphering what I felt God was trying to tell me to turn my business around, I applied *His instructions* to the best of my ability.

Lo and behold, my clients didn't abandon me, and I wound up having two of my best years ever. My hedge fund returned 117 percent net of all my performance fees. The message that was powerfully implanted in my mind that day was the best guidance I could have received. It saved my business, put food on the table for my family, and even afforded me a dream home in Bend, Oregon, the town I loved.

I often review these inspirational words from the Lord. I put 100 percent of my *trust* in Him. I take at least one hour of each day with Jesus to show the Lord that I *love* Him. I do my best to put Jesus Christ as the number one priority in my life, further demonstrating my love. I've read the Bible from front to back, and His *truth* has indeed *set me free*. Finally, I look inside of myself for the *answers* Jesus put in my heart, mind, and soul. Those words of instruction from the Lord are as powerful in my life today as they were many years ago when He gave them to me.

Does God Have a Sense of Humor?

> This is the day the Lord has made; let us rejoice and be glad in it. (Psalm 118:24 ESV)

In 2005, things went horribly wrong in my hedge fund, and in my life. I was making poor decisions, and I needed to get away from the office. I decided to go for a long hike by myself to think and pray. As I walked on the Deschutes River Trail in Central Oregon, I was in deep thought about all my recent difficulties. For a few seconds, I stopped walking and decided to pray: *God, please help me focus on this beautiful day even as I go through these difficult trials in my life. Amen.*

Lo and behold, I opened my eyes after finishing my prayer and instantly saw this giant pile of horse manure right in front of me. I chuckled and wondered how a pile of manure could be a sign from God on the beautiful day I mentioned in my prayer. But then I instantly realized that it was a life-lesson. As I started hiking again, I heard God speak these words into my heart, mind, and soul: **Along your path, beauty will be interrupted. Focus on My beauty.**

The timing of seeing that pile of manure just as I had asked God to take my mind off my troubles was impeccable. As I walked by the unpleasant site, God was telling me that one day my ugly pile of problems would also be behind me. I felt like God wanted me to understand that even as I deal with my problems, I must focus on His created beauty. I also felt God wanted me to find humor in my most difficult moments. On that lovely hike, I had a deep knowing that God was with me, and He would get me on the right path.

I went to that same hiking spot for the next several weeks, and each time, I noticed that the giant pile of manure got smaller and smaller until one day it was completely gone. Each day I went hiking on that path, I realized that over time, my current pile of problems would also get smaller and smaller. Lo and behold, over time, but not without struggle, the problems that plagued me on the hike were eventually gone.

In summary, I can say without a shadow of doubt that God helped me through each one of my problems until they completely faded away. I will always remember that hike as the day God comforted me by putting a big smile on my face. Finally, each day that I encounter a new pile of problems, I stay calm in knowing the Lord will guide me to a clear pathway where my ugly pile of problems will eventually disappear.

CHAPTER THREE

Instant Miracles

And all things, whatsoever ye shall ask in prayer, believing, ye shall receive.

—Matthew 21:22 KJV

As previously mentioned, I had two spectacular years in my hedge fund where I made a 79 percent gross return in 2003 and a 48 percent return in 2004. However, I made a bold decision in 2005 by taking a concentrated position in a low-priced stock in a company I will refer to as Eagle Entertainment. I made decent profits in Eagle Entertainment on the run-up to $7.00 per share from $2.00 when I first bought the stock.

My error in judgment was buying Eagle on the dip to $5.00, where I mistakenly believed the stock was a good buying opportunity. My biggest mistake was buying way too many shares. I wasn't in a normal state of mind when my buying spree of Eagle's stock was taking place. It all seemed to happen in a flash, and I felt horrible right after I completed my final purchase of the shares.

The good news was that even though I had bought one million shares, Eagle was trading several hundred thousand shares per day. This meant that over time I would have no problem selling the stock. However, a few days later, something surprising happened.

The stock started trading light volume, but at the same time, it was falling in price daily. Something strange was going on, but everyone I called on Wall Street had no idea why the stock was tanking.

Thirty days later, the stock was down 50 percent before the bad news finally came out. The company reported a horrible quarter, and they gave a weak profit outlook as well. Shortly after the bearish news hit the tape, Eagle's stock fell all the way back to $2.50 per share. I was devastated as my hedge funds performance got smashed.

My biggest dilemma was that the stock began trading only a few thousand shares per day while I owned one million shares. I went into a state of panic because I could have been forced to sell Eagle's stock at the market if my hedge fund investors demanded their money back. Any forced sales by me would have pushed Eagle Entertainments stock down another 50 percent or more. This is the problem with low-priced stocks as they often become roach motels, where you can get in (buy) but you can't get out (sell).

The worst part was there was little hope by the smart money investors that the stock would ever go up again. At this point, I hatched a plan. I decided to try selling Eagle to a bigger entertainment company to get my hedge fund investors liquid. I spoke to many potential acquirers, and in doing so, word of my plan was disclosed to the management of Eagle Entertainment.

This presented a new challenge. Upon hearing about my secretive plans, Eagle decided to issue a press release announcing a poison pill for shareholders to approve. A poison pill approval at the shareholder meeting would have prevented the takeover I was trying to create for the benefit of my hedge fund investors. After the poison pill was announced, I had about thirty days before the shareholders would approve the plan.

It was obvious to me that the best candidate to acquire Eagle Entertainment was a company that I will refer to as Big Cat Entertainment. I called the investor relations person at Big Cat because I didn't know anyone at the company. As a potential owner in Big Cat's stock, I asked him if I could stop by their headquarters and meet the management team. He agreed, and I showed up one week later.

Once I arrived, it was just me and the investor relations guy having a sandwich and talking about Big Cat's upcoming movie releases. I asked him if I could meet the CEO, and he said, "Sorry, Ron, management is in an all-hands meeting today." This was unfortunate because I was only in downtown Los Angeles for the day.

Fortunately for me, the IR guy got called out of our meeting. When he left, I immediately saw an opportunity. I went down the hall looking for the CEO of Big Cat Entertainment. I finally found his office with his assistant working there. I politely walked in and asked for her help. I said, "Would you please tell the CEO that I came all the way from Bend, Oregon, to hand him this letter?" She kindly agreed to do that for me. The letter, of course, was my takeout proposal of Eagle Entertainment by Big Cat Entertainment. I went back to the IR guy, thanked him for lunch, and left his office with a handful of movies.

God Works Behind the Scenes

Now this is where the story gets interesting. As I mentioned earlier, my time was running out because of the poison pill at the upcoming Eagle Entertainment shareholder meeting, which was only a few weeks away. When I returned to my office in Bend, I waited and waited, but no phone call was received from the CEO of Big Cat Entertainment.

When I had one week left before the Eagle Entertainment shareholder meeting, I realized that I needed a miracle for this deal to happen. I left my office and drove into a secluded place in the mountains to pray. It was early in the morning, and I was all alone with my Bible in the middle of the Deschutes National Forest sitting in my favorite backpacking chair when I prayed; *Heavenly Father, I desperately need your help. I believe my letter is sitting on the corner of the CEO's desk. My prayer is that if this is the case, you will nudge him to pick up the letter and read it. Amen.* I stayed in the woods for about two more hours before I returned to my office.

Lo and behold, as I walked up to my desk, I saw a yellow sticky from my assistant: "The CEO of Big Cat Entertainment just read your letter and would like you to call him ASAP." I was absolutely blown away! I called him immediately, and here's what the CEO said: "Ron, I've had your letter on the corner of my desk for a few weeks now but for some reason I felt the urge to pick it up and read it today. I like what you wrote. How should we proceed?"

Lo and behold, in just four days, we had our deal in place, and just in the nick of time. The $120 million acquisition was announced just days before the shareholder meeting, and Eagle Entertainment's stock erupted from $2.50 to $5.00 per share on the morning of the announcement. I was in Maui the day of the announcement where I received a bunch of phone calls from shareholders congratulating me. I had a lot of happy clients that sold their stock the day Eagle Entertainment's stock erupted 100 percent. It's amazing to me how God took a hopeless situation and turned it into the number one performing stock the day the deal was announced.

I must admit the deal I cut didn't work out for me the way I had hoped as the Big Cat Entertainment offer eventually fell apart. However, I did get the liquidity I desired. More importantly, I got to experience an instantly performed miracle! Not only did the miracle happen only a couple hours after I prayed, but it was confirmed by the CEO as to exactly how I prayed. The reality was that as hard as I had tried, I simply could not get an acquisition deal done by my own efforts. It wasn't until I intensely prayed for a miracle that my desired results happened. As Jesus said:

> I am the vine, ye are the branches: He that abideth
> in me, and I in him, the same bringeth forth much
> fruit: for without me ye can do nothing. If a man
> abide not in me, he is cast forth as a branch, and is
> withered; and men gather them, and cast them into
> the fire, and they are burned. If ye abide in me, and
> my words abide in you, ye shall ask what ye will,
> and it shall be done unto you. (John 15:5-7 KJV)

God Protects

> Save me, O God, by thy name, and judge me by thy strength. Hear my prayer, O God; give ear to the words of my mouth. For strangers are risen up against me, and oppressors seek after my soul: they have not set God before them. Selah. Behold, God is mine helper: The Lord is with them that uphold my soul. He shall reward evil unto mine enemies: cut them off in thy truth. I will freely sacrifice unto thee: I will praise thy name, O Lord; for it is good. For he hath delivered me out of all trouble: and mine eye hath seen his desire upon mine enemies. (Psalm 54:1–7 KJV)

After completing one of the biggest career accomplishments with the Big Cat Entertainment acquisition announcement, my hedge fund performance took a beating. Let me explain. As I mentioned earlier, God's direct intervention helped me to get Big Cat Entertainment to announce their intentions to acquire Eagle Entertainment. The good news was that I had convinced Big Cat Entertainment to swap my illiquid Eagle Entertainment stock into Big Cat's liquid stock at a hefty premium in my favor. The bad news was that I received restricted shares in Big Cat Entertainment, which meant I had to hold the stock for six months. Legally, I could not lock in my unrealized profits by hedging my restricted shares of Big Cat. In other words, I was at the complete mercy of Big Cat Entertainments stock performance over the course of six months.

As I mentioned earlier, most Eagle Entertainment shareholders profited handsomely because once the acquisition deal was announced by Big Cat Entertainment, Eagle Entertainment's stock erupted 100 percent. My clients were smart shareholders that took full advantage of the price jump and sold their Eagle shares on the day of the Big Cat announcement. If I did not swap all of my Eagle Entertainment stock for Big Cat's stock, I too would have sold my remaining Eagle shares the minute the news of the proposed acquisition was announced. In fact, that's exactly what I suggested everyone else do when I was asked after the news announcement.

The bad news for me was that Big Cat Entertainment had a couple box office disappointments over the six months that I was restricted to sell. The other bad news was that a negative research report on Big Cat Entertainment was circulated around Wall Street. This report predicted Big Cat's stock would implode. All of this added up to the stock falling from $11 to below $8 per share the day I was able to legally sell Big Cat's stock. This put my hedge fund back into a loss position.

Most of my hedge fund investors appreciated my efforts in helping get Big Cat Entertainment to acquire Eagle Entertainment. They also understood I had bad luck with the six month restriction. However, I ran into some legal problems as not everyone was pleased with my efforts.

God Is Just

And whatsoever ye shall ask in my name, that will
I do, that the Father may be glorified in the Son.
(John 14:13 KJV)

This is where the story gets interesting from a spiritual perspective. I was sitting alone in my office, and I got a call from my attorney in Bend. He said, "Ron, I have some bad news. I was just told there is no way to settle this dispute and that you will be thrown into court. At this point, Ron, I'm sorry to tell you, but this will cost you another $100,000 for me to defend you, and it will probably cost you another year of your life. Since you don't have the money, I'll have to wish you good luck at this point."

The reality was that the hedge fund losses also hit me extremely hard. I had 95 percent of my liquid net worth in the fund. After the fund's performance was crushed, I took another hit with a giant tax bill. Then, add in the fact that my legal bills piled up fast, and I had a wife and three kids to feed. The bottom line is that I didn't have the $100,000 to defend myself, and this resulted in my attorney politely stepping aside. After I hung up the phone with him, I was devastated. The last thing I needed was a lost year of my life in a legal entanglement. I desperately wanted to put all of this behind me and get on with my life. The comment that worried me the most was when my attorney said at the very end of our call: "Ron, anything can happen if this case goes in front of a jury."

Jesus Is Listening

> And it shall come to pass, that before they call, I will answer; and while they are yet speaking, I will hear. (Isaiah 65:24 KJV)

I had this small Jesus plaque hanging on my office wall. I grabbed it and went back to my desk. I held it close to my chest as I prayed with my eyes closed, and my head down: *Jesus, I know You can protect me and my family. I'm praying and believing with all my heart You will give me a miracle and make this nightmare go away. Amen.*

The Phone Rang!

Lo and behold, right after I finished my prayer, the phone rang! It was my dear friend Tom McChesney. I said, "Hi Tom, what's up?"

He said, "I was just thinking about you."

I said, "Tom, I need to tell you something." I proceeded to tell him what my attorney just said and after I finished, I said, "Tom, I believe you have my answer to get me out of this mess."

He replied, "Ron, I don't think I do, but I'm sorry about what you are going through."

I was convinced Tom had the answer to my prayer. I said, "Tom, please think. Is there anyone you can think of that could possibly help me?"

He thought for a minute and said, "Call my friend Keith, who is an attorney that helped me in the past."

I quickly called Keith knowing that he was the instrument of my answered prayer.

When I called, Keith asked me to tell him the whole story, which I did. He said, "Ron, I'm afraid you're in a mess that will cost you at least $100,000 in legal fees. It sounds like you don't have the money, so I don't know how I can help."

Lo and behold, he then asked me the magic question; "Who is the attorney on the other side?" I told him the gentlemen's name. He said, "Are you kidding me? He is one of my tenants in the building I own. In fact, he is one of my best friends and we are meeting for lunch in five minutes. Call me back in a couple hours because I can get this legal issue resolved for you."

As you can imagine, I was absolutely blown away! I called back a couple hours later, and here's what Keith said: "Ron, be at my office on Monday because I'll have this whole thing resolved for you."

I asked Keith how much it would cost, and he said he would do it free of charge. When we hung up, I became overwhelmingly filled with the Holy Spirit as I prayed, *Jesus, thank You so much for Your supernatural power and for this instant miracle. Amen.*

On Monday, as promised, Keith solved the whole matter. It was not only a miracle that happened but an *instant miracle*. For you skeptics, ask yourself this question: What are the odds of this randomly happening? The fact of the matter is that by divine intervention I received a powerful miracle that protected me.

> Behold, God is mine helper: the Lord is with them that uphold my soul. He shall reward evil unto mine enemies: cut them off in thy truth. (Psalm 54:4–5 KJV)

Jesus Performs Wondrous Signs

> It has seemed good to me to show the signs and wonders that the Most-High God has done for me. How great are his signs, how mighty his wonders! His kingdom is an everlasting kingdom, and his dominion endures from generation to generation. (Daniel 4:2–3 ESV)

Many of you who read the previous phone-ringing God story might have some lingering doubts about it being a divinely inspired supernatural event. This next story, which is a follow-up to the previous one, just might convince you that Jesus is alive, and He listens to heartfelt prayers of those who love and trust Him with all their hearts.

The Phone Rang Again!

> He will fulfil the desire of them that fear him: he also will hear their cry, and will save them. (Psalm 145:19 KJV)

The good news in the previous God story was that the Lord spared me the embarrassment of defending myself in a court of law. But here's the bad news: The hedge fund losses, the attorney bills, the lack of income, being unemployed, and the legal settlement all left me broke. After getting my legal challenge behind me, I was back at my office in Winthrop, Washington, realizing that I had no money for groceries, gas, or rent. All I could think about was the fact that I was unemployed and the sole provider for a family of five. It was an awful feeling, but I knew just what to do. I put my head down on the desk, and prayed; *"Dear Lord, thank You for protecting me, but now I'm in desperate need of Your help to feed my family. I'm asking You for another miracle. Amen.*

Lo and behold, the phone rang after I finished praying! The second I picked up the phone, I knew it was my answered prayer. It was a former client of mine named Alan. He said, "Ron, I just inherited $30,000, and I was wondering if you had a good investment idea for me."

I said, "Alan, I own a large chunk of shares in a private company that's currently doing a private offering at $5.00 per share. I'd be willing to sell you my thirty thousand shares at $1 per share. In fact, I'll sell you all of my shares and my warrants for $30,000.00. If you're interested, I'll put you in touch with the CEO. Then, you can determine for yourself if you want to take me up on my offer."

Lo and behold, Alan called me back a few days later and wired $30,000 into my bank account! This was a win-win for both of us as he got a huge discount on all of my private shares, and I received money that I desperately needed. Most importantly, Jesus Christ had just performed another Instant miracle! Not more than a few seconds after finishing my prayer did the phone ring, and it was the perfect answer to my prayer! To say Jesus answered me again would be an incredible understatement. This miracle not only put food on the table, but it also helped me pay travel expenses to put together a new business deal in Medford, Oregon.

> For to us a child is born, to us a son is given; and the government shall be upon his shoulder, and his name shall be called Wonderful Counselor, Mighty God, Everlasting Father, Prince of Peace. (Isaiah 9:6 ESV)

CHAPTER FOUR

God Speaks

I sought the Lord, and he heard me, and delivered me from all my fears.

—Psalm 34:4 KJV

Back in 2005, the real estate market was red hot. I hoped to take advantage of the overvalued market when I put my house up for sale. I had decided to leave the area once my legal problems surfaced. I was worried about the implications of a trial while living in a small town. I wanted to protect my family, but where would we go? There was only one thing for me to do. I went to the river to pray.

I sat by my favorite river looking at the beauty that surrounded me. I prayed; *Thank You Father, for giving me eyes to see Your created beauty, and ears to hear the wonderful sounds of nature all around me. As You know, I'm under duress from this lawsuit. I need someplace safe to go, preferably far away. Lord, I need a place where I can recover my peace of mind to solve my problems, but where should I go? Amen.*

Lo and behold, I heard one word whispered into my mind: **Winthrop.** I knew little about Winthrop, Washington, except that it was known as a good place to go hut-to-hut cross country skiing. Upon hearing Winthrop, I immediately investigated. I looked on the internet and saw a picture of downtown Winthrop, which looked like an old cowboy town.

A few days after my answered prayer, my daughter, Anna, and I drove several hours north to Winthrop. It turned out to be one of the nicest car trips I've ever had as my daughter and I had a great time on our four-day round-trip. As we entered the tiny town of Winthrop, Anna said, "Dad, this is a beautiful area, but we certainly can't live here as it's out in the middle of nowhere." However, we had so much fun exploring the area that I started to think Winthrop was exactly where the family needed to be.

The real estate agent showed us all around the area where we saw a bunch of homes for sale. At the end of a long day, I realized that houses in the Methow Valley of Winthrop were incredibly overvalued. I asked the real estate agent if there were any rentals, and he assured me that there were none and that homes in Winthrop are rarely ever available to rent. Upon hearing the disappointing news, we returned home.

After arriving back home, my first thought was, now what? As you might expect, I decided to go back to the exact same place on the river where God sent Winthrop into my mind. Once again, I prayed; *Father in heaven, there are no homes to rent, yet I felt You put Winthrop into my mind. What am I to do now? Amen.*

Lo and behold, the answer came immediately: **Call the other one.** It took me a few minutes until I figured out what that instruction from the Lord meant. But then I realized that there were only two real estate agencies in the tiny town of Winthrop, which had a population of 400 people. I took the Chamber of Commerce material I gathered from the trip, and I called **the other** real estate agent.

A nice young lady answered. I explained to her that I didn't want to give any false impressions as I had already met with her competitor. Of course, she knew the other Realtor in town, and she even went to high school with his daughter. I explained to her that the other agent told me there's never anything available to rent in

Winthrop. She agreed that the rental market was almost nonexistent in the Methow Valley.

Lo and behold, she says, "Believe it or not, we just got a beautiful home to list for rent today. The owner of the home got reassigned to Seattle but doesn't want to sell the house as he hopes to retire in Winthrop, and the house for rent is beautiful and in one of the best locations in the Methow Valley." She continued, "The best part, he only wants $1,100 per month for his custom designed home. I'll email you all the information with pictures right now."

This was amazing timing, God's perfect timing. The next day I packed all three kids and we headed off to see the house. When we arrived, I was blown away. It was a stunning home with gorgeous mountain views. I fell in love with it, and the owner said he would rent the house to me for the two years I requested. Within a few weeks, we did a partial move into our beautiful new home in Winthrop, Washington!

I can tell you this, I couldn't have thought of a more wholesome place for my kids to experience, as the area was quiet, safe, secluded, and stunning. Certainly, there was no better place on earth for me to have an opportunity to clear my mind and solve my problems. I know without a shadow of a doubt that God spoke to my mind, and because I listened, He rewarded me with all that I had asked for in my prayers.

God Will Speak Directly to Your Heart

A righteous man may have many troubles, but the Lord delivers him from them all. (Psalm 34:19 NIV)

When I closed my business, I was devastated. I remember thinking I should leave the financial industry and look for a new career. However, after analyzing my situation carefully, I realized I had too much knowledge of the equity markets to simply walk away. Even though I felt discouraged, I knew I had more to do in the financial services industry.

I said a prayer and asked God what I should do. I felt like God wanted me to write a book about the future of the stock market. The problem with writing a book at this point in my life was that I was unemployed. In other words, I had serious doubts about the timing and feasibility of writing a book. First, I never published anything, and second, I was at the lowest point in my financial career as I had just closed my hedge fund down. Doubts about writing a financial book weighed heavily on my mind, so I decided to pray with this Bible verse in mind: "Therefore I say unto you, What things soever ye desire, when ye pray, believe ye receive them, and ye shall have them (Mark 11:24 KJV)

Instantly Answered Prayers

I was in my office in Winthrop filled with confusion because I felt God put this desire to write a book upon my heart. I prayed: *Lord; am I supposed to write a book?* At that moment, I immediately decided to do a random Bible opening. A random Bible opening is where I pick up my Bible, close my eyes in prayer, flip the Bible around in my hands, and open it with the full expectation for an answer from God.

Lo and behold, my index finger went to the very top of the page of the Old Testament in Jeremiah 29:31 where I read these three words: **send this message.**

Immediately after I read, *send this message,* it seemed abundantly clear to me this was a direct answer to my prayer. However, the next day, nagging doubts filled my mind. In the same place in my office, I prayed again; *Lord, am I really supposed to write a book?* At that moment, I instinctively felt God instruct me to go back and read more of Jeremiah for my final answer.

Lo and behold, I opened to where I had read in Jeremiah the day before, and the very next passage, right below the previous one—Jeremiah 30:2–3 NIV: **"Write in a book all the words I have spoken to you. The days are coming, declares the Lord."**

Now, you've got to understand that it wasn't just the direct answer to my specific question in that prayer (write in a book) that blew my mind. It was also the words; "The days are coming." You see, it was early 2007, and I was thinking about writing a book about a coming collapse in the global economy. The combination of these two sentences got my full attention. The final decision to write the book was made right then and there. I took my twenty years of experience and typed all my thoughts on my computer.

Most people thought it was a total waste of time writing a book because I would certainly not get published. Second, the predications I was making seemed ludicrous. Not only was I calling for a stock market collapse and a real estate market crash, but I also predicted gold would erupt in price from the Federal Reserve's massive money printing.

My predictions seemed outrageous because real estate had been in a fifty-year bull market. In fact, outside of the Great Depression, real estate had never fallen in every state simultaneously like I was predicting. Stocks had also been in a long-running bull market while gold was a hated relic by most Wall Street experts. Stocks were on a tear as the Dow Jones Industrial Average hit all-time highs as I started typing my book.

After several months of typing and editing, the manuscript was officially completed. I decided to self-publish my book as suggested by Robert Allen in his audiotape program titled *The Road to Wealth.* In December 2007, I went to a self-publishing warehouse called Maverick Publishing in Bend, Oregon, to make five hundred copies of my new self-published paperback book: *Discover the Upside of Down.* I completed my self-published book close to the very top of the stock market. In other words, that book was published with near perfect timing because in January 2008 the stock market started a horrific bear market, and it all started the day my five hundred self-published books were printed. God taught me that His timing is always perfect.

God Speaks in Different Ways

I sought the Lord, and He heard me, And delivered
me from all my fears. (Psalm 34:4 NKJV)

A few weeks after receiving the five hundred copies of my book, I
was sitting in my office one night reflecting on the fact that I could
not get any media attention. This was because I was "only" a self-
published author. I needed to get a respectable book publisher if I
was going to get any traction with national TV and radio. I took out
an index card where I wrote down my new goal: *Get a major book
publishing company to publish my book.*

As I sat there looking at my new goal, I asked myself, how does
a person who has never written any published material attract a
reputable book publisher? I was at my office late at night when I put
my head down on the desk and prayed about my dilemma: *Dear
God, please help me find a book publisher. Amen.*

Lo and behold, the Lord answered instantly: **Turn Around**.

When I turned around, I saw my bookshelf directly behind me
where all my books on the stock market were placed. I immediately
knew to review those books to find the right publishing company. I
noticed my favorite books, written by the most famous stock market
traders, were mostly published by John Wiley & Sons. God gave me
the perfect answer, which was to reach out to John Wiley & Sons.

God Guides His Believers

As one might expect, God answered my prayer in a big way as
he sent me to the world's largest publisher of financial books. As
I scrolled around the John Wiley & Sons website, I found a lady
named Jennifer who specialized in books written about the stock
market. My initial thought was she probably gets hundreds of emails
and phone calls each week from aspiring authors. I wondered how

I could stand out from the others. Funny enough, my cousin Dave had just signed me up for video email capabilities with a multilevel marketing company called Hello-World. I decided to send Jennifer a video email of me holding up my new book. Here is what I said:

> Hello, my name is Ron Coby. I'm holding in my hand the timeliest book in the world today. In this self-published book, I predict real estate markets and stock markets around the globe are set to crash. I predict gold is going to explode much higher. This book is 100 percent complete, fully edited by two college professors, and ready to hit bookstores now. I decided to contact the world's largest book publisher of financial books first because you published the best market books of all-time. Call or email me right away because I'm going to work my way down the list of available book publishers.

Jennifer called me the very next day! She asked me to overnight five books. Lo and behold, a few weeks later, I had a publishing contract signed with the world's largest book publisher! I was filled with excitement about becoming a published author. In less than two years, I went from closing my money management business to becoming a published author doing interviews on national television. This was all thanks to God powerfully answering my prayer that resulted in an instant miracle.

Let's do a quick retake. God answered my question in a prayer about writing a book. He answered the first time in a random Bible opening with: **send this message**. Then, for clear confirmation of what he instructed, the very next day he sent me back to the Bible where it said: **write in a book**. To top it all off, when I asked God in a prayer for a book publisher, He answered me instantly with **Turn Around** and sent me to the world's largest publisher of financial books. One clear lesson that I learned in all of this is that goal setting backed by the power of prayer is the most impactful thing a person can do to change his or her world. As the New Testament says, "I can do all things through Christ which strengtheneth me" Philippians 4:13 (KJV).

God Wants the Best for All His Children

Have not I commanded thee? Be strong and of good courage; be not afraid, neither be thou dismayed: for the Lord thy God is with thee whithersoever thou goest. (Joshua 1:9 KJV)

Getting a book contract did indeed change my world as it helped me put together a business deal that I had been working on for several months. The publishing contract also put me on a grand new adventure where I was on national, regional, and local TV and radio. I was also quoted in several of my favorite financial publications. The media coverage, the book publishing contract, and a new business partnership all resulted from my preset goals backed by the power of prayer. It was remarkable how far God had taken me in such a short period of time. It was only a couple years earlier I was distraught about closing my business. God took me from my pathetic situation to becoming a published author on national television. *Thank You God for answering my prayers, and for doing it in such a spectacular fashion! Amen.*

CHAPTER FIVE

God Heals

> If we confess our sins, he is faithful and just to forgive
> us our sins and purify us from all unrighteousness.
>
> **—1 John 1:9 NIV**

I set a specific goal to help my clients by selling our investment in Connectsoft Inc. to a larger company. Specifically, Connectsoft was a private corporation where there was no way to liquidate our private shares in an open market transaction on a national stock exchange like the NYSE or NASDAQ. The only way to get a return on the illiquid investment was to go public and list the shares on a national stock exchange or sell Connectsoft to another publicly traded corporation for cash or stock.

In 2006, I tried to sell Connectsoft to three different public companies that were all interested in their proprietary software. The CEO of Connectsoft felt the timing for a sale wasn't good, but I told him we needed to sell the company before the economy went into a recession. I knew Connectsoft wouldn't survive an economic downturn let alone the global collapse I was anticipating. Even if Connectsoft did survive a recession, I was sure that our equity would get completely wiped out through a process called dilution. As a result of our disagreement, the CEO and I had a falling out where I told him to only contact me again when the company was either sold or shut down.

Sure enough, Connectsoft had to take on an unhealthy level of burdensome debt to stay alive during the recession in 2008. And like I suspected; the debt essentially wiped out our equity position. My two biggest fears were realized when the economy collapsed, and my clients equity in Connectsoft evaporated.

In 2010, I was sitting at my desk and praying. I heard Jesus speak to my heart to call the CEO of Connectsoft and apologize to him. The Lord apparently didn't want me harboring any bad feelings. He also knew my goal for several years was to get the company liquid for my clients. I picked up the phone shortly after I prayed and called the CEO. I told him I was sorry for our falling out because it was ultimately his decision to make about the timing of the sale of the company. He quickly forgave me and showed me a demonstration of his exciting new prototype software called QWARK.

A month later, the CEO asked me if I would raise him $2 million on a note offering. He also asked me to help him sell the company to get the shareholders a return on their investment. My business partner and I jumped on the opportunity. We wound up raising Connectsoft $3 million, and we had a big payday as a result.

Lo and behold, nine months later, Connectsoft was sold to one of the largest chipmakers in the world. My investors made a quick 100 percent return on the note offering. Wonderfully enough, I played a critical role in making the acquisition successful. My long-held goal had finally been accomplished when Connectsoft was sold.

In summary, I believe the Lord was rewarding me for listening to His command put upon my heart to call and apologize to the CEO. Jesus not only rewarded me with a nice payday but more importantly, He also helped me accomplish a goal I had set many years earlier. It's amazing to me how it appeared hopeless that my goal to liquidate Connectsoft would ever be realized. However, a simple act of forgiveness resulted in a restored relationship with the CEO, an important goal of mine being accomplished, and big profits for my investors. Here's the point of the story: God speaks to our hearts, and He rewards us for listening to Him.

God Fixes

> For where two or three are gathered together in my name, there am I in the midst of them. (Matthew 18:20 KJV)

One day while eating pizza, my tooth cracked. The next day, I went to see a dentist for an X-ray. I was informed that I needed to get a root canal because of the decay in my tooth. Apparently, the decay was the main reason my tooth cracked in the first place. I told her I was in a tight spot financially and I couldn't afford a root canal. She said, "Then you're going to be in excruciating pain." I asked, "How long do I have?" She responded, "I'd say two months, and when it happens, you'll need medication because the pain will be intense."

As she predicted, two months later I woke up with an incredible amount of pain all around the cracked tooth in the back of my mouth. Of course, I remembered what the dentist said about calling her for pain medication. However, I still had no money or dental insurance. I decided to have my best friend Joni pray with me about the tooth. For several months Joni lived in southern Oregon while I lived in Central Oregon. We decided that each day at 7:30 a.m. we would pray at the exact same time. The morning after my mouth was full of pain, we each prayed specifically for my healing.

God Relieves Pain

Lo and behold, the very next morning after we prayed, my toothache was all gone! The pain stayed away for a few months, but then it started to act up again. Of course, I decided to pray. Unbelievable enough, a few hours later, something wild happened. I was reading when suddenly, another little piece of that same tooth fell out of my mouth. Lo and behold, I spat it out into my hand, and I was immediately relieved of all discomfort!

As I evaluated my pain relief, it's my belief that having the extra tiny piece of tooth out of my mouth had somehow relieved the pressure off my gums. I'm not a dentist, but apparently the Lord acted as one upon my behalf as one year from the initial visit to the dentist, my tooth was still cracked but with no pain. Once I got back on my feet financially, I went to the dentist for my root canal.

Now, here's my supernatural explanation from the Bible: For where two or three are gathered in my name, there am I in the midst of them. Here's the bottom line; Joni and I prayed together, and Jesus answered our prayers and He gave me comfort when I most desperately needed it.

God Changes Hearts

> Again I say to you that if two of you agree on earth concerning anything that they ask, it will be done for them by My Father in heaven. For where two or three are gathered together in My name, I am there in the midst of them. (Matthew 18:19–20 NKJV)

To say my life has been a roller coaster ride would be a gross understatement. It just so happened that in 2012, both my marriage and my business partnership ended. I was left with a huge amount of business debts and no job or savings. In essence, I was broke and nearly homeless, living with friends or family. This story begins when a distant relative who I'll refer to as my cousin Billy, allowed me to live with him in his home.

The first day I moved in, Billy was agitated with me. It started off with him nitpicking every single move I made and oftentimes he became upset. This went on for a couple months until it became unbearable for both of us. Joni suggested that we pray specifically for Billy to be kind to me. I told Joni it would literally take a miracle to turn my cousin around from his bullying behavior.

The next morning after we prayed, Billy was the angriest he had ever been toward me. In fact, he belittled me as he left for work and told me to pack up and leave, which meant I would soon be homeless. This was not what I was expecting the first day after Joni and I prayed for him to be kind to me! To make matters worse, my car had recently been repossessed because I had no money to make my payments. As I was getting ready to leave his house to walk to an unknown destination, I decided to send my cousin a series of texts. I shamed him by saying that if his mother were still alive, she would never have approved of his bad treatment of me by literally sending me to the streets.

Lo and behold, Billy felt badly and texted me a sincere apology. He said that he was a loner and that he underestimated how hard it would be to live with somebody. He admitted how horrible he felt for his treatment of me and promised it would end. When he came home later that evening, he said that he was deeply sorry for treating me poorly.

Lo and behold, when he arrived home, he asked me if I wanted one of his favorite beers. I agreed, and he proceeded to open the beer, and he even brought it to me! Trust me, this had never happened before. Amazingly enough, Billy and I had our best conversation in all the months we had lived together. Surprisingly, he offered me a second beer and opened that one for me too. And even more wonderfully, Billy treated me with respect for the remaining five weeks that I lived with him.

This was an extreme turnaround and an instant miracle since it happened one day after Joni and I simultaneously prayed together at

7:30 a.m. This miracle showed me that God can change a person's heart. God can also change troubled circumstances like mine, and He can do it quickly.

> The righteous cry, and the Lord heareth, and delivereth them out of all their troubles. (Psalm 34:17 KJV)

God Listens, Answers, and Confirms

In early 2014, my father was diagnosed with lymphoma. The doctors decided chemotherapy was his only option for survival. They told him he wouldn't have long to live unless he started chemo because the cancer was worsening. My dad eventually listened to his doctor's advice and did his first chemo session. Apparently, he responded well to the treatment, and his red and white blood cells slightly improved.

Shortly thereafter, my dad suffered from a lung issue that halted his remaining chemo treatments. In fact, my dad could hardly breathe and he was coughing up blood. When I arrived at his hospital bed, my dad was extremely sick. His doctor had serious concerns that he would not survive from the one-two punch of cancer spreading along with a debilitating lung disease. Fortunately, the doctor decided to take out a piece of my dad's lung and discovered he had an extremely rare condition called bronchiolitis obliterans organizing pneumonia (BOOP). Once this lung disorder was accurately diagnosed, the doctors changed his medication. Several weeks later he was experiencing some relief from this debilitating lung disease, but he needed to live with a breathing machine.

I needed to head back to Central Oregon. I felt horrible leaving my dad because he looked half-dead in his hospital bed when I departed. Each day I checked in to see how he was doing. The battle with cancer was extremely difficult for him. He was having a hard time getting out of bed, and he was losing far too much weight. Fortunately, my dad had a supportive wife with friends and family praying for him.

One day, I went to my favorite spot on the beautiful Metolius River in Sisters, Oregon. I hiked all afternoon and spent most of that time praying for my dad to be healed. I stopped to pray at the most serene spots near the river on a sunny day. I felt confident God heard my prayers. In fact, I had felt His presence while I prayed and became very peaceful about my dad's dire situation with BOOP and lymphoma.

Shortly thereafter, my dad's BOOP got under control and the doctor allowed him to go home. To help him breathe, he used a special breathalyzer during the day and an oxygen tank at night. He was also rescheduled for a series of six outpatient chemo treatments. Each day I spoke to my dad I could hear in his voice that he was slowly feeling a little bit better. After a daily regimen of rehab, he was soon able to walk. In my heart, I felt like God was slowly healing him. Once again, I went on a hike, praying intensely for Jesus to heal my dad completely.

The Phone Rang!

Several days later, as I left the house for a hike, the phone rang, and it was my dad. He said, "Ronnie, I went to start my next scheduled chemo treatment today. However, after a series of tests, the doctor told me the cancer is all gone, and I'm in remission." At that moment, I said, "Dad, God listened to everyone's prayers and healed you!" Lo and behold, while I was nearly speechless on the phone with my dad, I noticed that a call was coming in on my cell phone. I told my dad I would call him right back. On the screen of my phone, I saw the call was from Alan. He was the person who God used to grant me an instant miracle a few years earlier when I desperately needed money.

After seeing Alan's name on the cell phone, I recalled the instant miracle I had with him several years earlier. I immediately knew God answered my prayers and He just confirmed the remission miracle for my dad! I had further confirmation as my body erupted with a multitude of powerful emotions: tears welled up in my eyes, and my entire being was overflowing with the power of the Holy Spirit. The call from my dad was awesome in itself. However, the confirmation call from Alan as my dad had just told me about his miracle, hit me like a ton of bricks.

I was overwhelmed as I felt like I was engulfed with the presence of the Lord. It was like I was having an out-of-body experience as I was completely covered with the Holy Spirit. It was as if a shield of perfect love engulfed me. It didn't take but a second after seeing Alan's name on my cell phone to absolutely know, beyond a shadow of a doubt, that God heard my prayers and confirmed His remission miracle.

I asked Alan why he called me, and he said he just wanted to see how I was doing. Once I gathered myself, I told him the entire miracle story and that his call was my confirmation from God. He said, "Well, Ron, what are you going to do about it?" After we hung up, I did the only thing I could think of, and that was to pray. As I hiked into a sandy forest area of the high desert where I have never hiked before, I prayed: *God, thank You for my dad's remission miracle, and thank You for confirming this amazing miracle. I'm here to ask what You would have me do to honor You. I will walk and listen. Amen.*

Lo and behold, while I was all alone peacefully walking in the high desert plains of Central Oregon, a still small voice said: **Write it All in a Book.**

In summary, what you have been reading is the direct result of what God spoke to my heart the day of His remission miracle. My dad went on to have two months of perfect health in his remission from cancer. The sequence of events that included my dad telling me of his miracle cure, and then Alan's confirmation-call, happened to be one of the most powerful experiences of my life. By the way, my answered prayer from God's granted miracle sent me off on a spiritual journey with Him that makes up the remainder of this book. At this point, God was about to take me on a whole new walk with Him filled with all kinds of unexpected new miracles and spectacular supernatural events.

CHAPTER SIX

God Speaks in Different Ways

Ask, and it shall be given you; seek, and ye shall find; knock, and it shall be opened unto you.

—Matthew 7:7 KJV

When God instructed me to write this book, I set out on a bold mission: Put my faith to the test by proving God, with His Son Jesus Christ, can communicate with His people through answered prayers and created miracles, even instant miracles. Even though I've had so many powerful miracles manifest in my life, I had no idea how to approach this seemingly impossible mission. However, I knew the Lord would deliver because He said, "with man this is impossible, but with God all things are possible."

I felt that a current proof-statement of new miracles was needed to complete this book by showing God's power in the present moment. As I made this miracle request in my prayers, I showed God how much I believed in His power and the power of His Son to perform miracles in my life. Why wouldn't I make this bold decision to ask God to perform new miracles after already experiencing so many supernatural events? Honestly, it was the only logical decision to make, especially as I started typing this book.

God Empowers His People

My new spiritual adventure started as I looked at the Bible verse from Jeremiah on an index card that I carried around for many years: "Call unto Me, and I will answer you, and show you great and mighty things, which you do not know" (Jeremiah 33:3 NKJV).

I was frustrated trying to build subscribers for my financial newsletter called *The Coby Report*. I was offering hedge fund managers a free two-week trial of my stock timing report. I felt confident they would give me a try after seeing my performance numbers, but I couldn't get many fund managers on the phone. I was either being screened by the fund manager's personal assistant, or I was leaving voice messages all over Wall Street.

My frustration after sixty days of failed attempts left me with the decision to change my sales strategy as cold calling was not working. I decided to sit down and do an honest evaluation of my past business successes and failures. This was an enlightening process because it was clear to me that I needed to have God behind all my goals and in front of everything I do. The reason was simple. Whenever I prayed intensely, God listened and sometimes, He even responded instantaneously.

I decided to write new goals and review old ones to get inspired. My new specific goals fell under the following categories: spiritual awareness, physical health, emotional well-being, healthy relationships, financial freedom, and wisdom. The one goal that stuck out was wisdom because it was obvious, I needed much more of God's wisdom in my life. I decided to make God my number one priority. Due to my frustration, I decided to say an intense prayer.

Lord, thank You for all my blessings. As You know, I decided to make You my number one priority in life. I'm sorry that I have not made this decision sooner. I've decided I must dig deep into the Word to acquire true wisdom. I'm going to open my Bible randomly and ask that You show me what I need to learn right now. I'm asking You to teach me Your wisdom in all my remaining days ahead. Amen.

Lo and behold, after flipping the Bible all around in my hands and with my eyes closed, I did my random Bible opening to Ecclesiastes where my index finger went right next to the very first sentence of Ecclesiastes in my Joyce Meyer *Everyday Life Bible* where she said: "Solomon the wise King wrote Ecclesiastes. He realized that everything on earth is an exercise in vanity if we do not fear God and obey His word."

Solomon was considered the wisest man in the Old Testament and one of the wisest men to ever live. As you might expect, this random Bible opening, like the previous one, couldn't have been more perfect in relation to the prayer I had just finished. The message was clear: All my actions were in vain unless God and His Word were wrapped around everything I do. It was also obvious to me that random Bible openings would be an important way the Lord will communicate with me in helping me finish this book.

Many of you reading all of this might pass this off as a coincidence but I can tell you beyond all doubt that this experience, and the ones you are about to read, were not mere coincidences. It was God meeting me in the present moment. After many instant miracles and multiple random Bible openings in my life, I'm convinced God wants to have a relationship with his children through the power of Jesus Christ and the Holy Spirit, and He wants to communicate in the here and now. I was so convinced that it became clear that God wanted to communicate with me in a way that He had performed in the past.

With all this in mind, I decided to do my random Bible opening each morning near the end of my Hour of Spiritual Power. It was this hour of dedication to God where I would read from my Bible along with several of my favorite Christian books and then journal about the miracles that happened. You be the judge as I share more coincidences that I call supernatural experiences. Here's what I wrote in the very beginning of this book, or what I call the start of my new spiritual journey with God.

Putting my Faith to the Test

October 26

On day one, I specifically prayed for an answer for my struggling business. Lo and behold, a few hours later my cousin called. "Ron, I've got it! I have found the answer to kick start your business." The timing was impeccable as he shared with me some wonderful new internet marketing ideas and strategies.

October 27

A friend of mine texted me saying she was very sick. She was a single mom who couldn't afford to miss any work. I specifically prayed for her to get well by Monday morning. Lo and behold, I get a text from her saying; "Your prayers worked! I'm feeling 100% better and I was able to go to work this morning. Thank-you so much!"

October 28

My finances ran low. In fact, I couldn't afford my November rent. I prayed and asked God to provide the money. Lo and behold, the very day I prayed, Karen Davis, a good friend of mine, texted me: "Ron, whatever you need me to do, I will help." A few days later, November's rent was wired by Karen directly to the landlord.

October 29

My dad was extremely sick, and at this moment in time, he was in the hospital suffering from severe kidney problems. I prayed and asked God to alleviate his kidney issues. Lo and behold, a few days later, my dad called. "Ronnie, I'm heading home from the hospital as my kidney issues are gone."

October 30

After looking back in detail over the course of my life, I still felt a lack of desire. It occurred to me that I'm a much different person in my fifties than I was as a driven young man. I prayed and specifically asked God to help me uncover my desire to become more motivated. Lo and behold, I looked out my window and noticed one of the most beautiful sunrises I'd ever seen.

I felt directed to go for a walk on the Deschutes River Trail, which I had never done at the crack of dawn. On that early morning hike, I noticed five curious otters swimming right next to me making loud grunting noises. It was as if they were trying to communicate with me. Then, out of nowhere, several loud geese flew right next to me and over the otters in the river. The next thing I know, a lovely blue bird sat on a branch next to where I was standing. Then, I heard a squirrel squawking at me as I was looking at the spectacular sunrise glowing brightly. It was like God had His creation speaking to my heart.

Lo and behold, it hit me like a ton of bricks; this is exactly what brings me joy and motivates me to be self-employed. Having the ability to hike whenever I want on a beautiful river trail is not something I would likely do if I had to punch the clock from nine-to-five. I could clearly see that if I continue to work hard for myself, I will always be able to do things like a beautiful nature walk whenever I desire. I decided to use this God-created experience in nature as a reminder to get motivated each day.

Once again, I asked, and God answered perfectly by sending me into His created beauty. God touched my soul with a family of curious otters, a flock of noisy geese, a lovely blue bird, a rowdy squirrel, and a beautiful sunrise. What an awesome God!

October 31

For several days I had been thinking about where I would go to live once the lease on my Bend condo was up at year-end. I long held this idea that I would go live in a cool little western ski town for the winter. Lo and behold, I had breakfast with my landlord. He just happened to mention the little ski town I had my eye on. I asked him what he thought about it and to compare it to Bend, Oregon, where we both lived. He had several negative things to say about the other town. I took this as a clear sign not to move there. For me, this wasn't just a mere coincidence because God knew this was under serious consideration, as the decision had been weighing on my heart. While the landlord spoke despairingly about the little ski town, God used this person to help make the decision for me.

This left the question; should I just stay in the beautiful mountain town of Bend, Oregon? In my heart, I felt like it was time to leave as I had lived in Bend, on and off, for many years. Even though I absolutely loved the area, I felt like I should try a new place. After breakfast, I decided to go back to my condo and pray. I asked God what his thoughts were about the events of the morning and where I should go.

Lo and behold, with my eyes closed, I flipped the Bible around in my hands and did my random Bible opening in my Joyce Meyer *Everyday Life Bible* to Deuteronomy 1:6: "You have dwelt long enough on this mountain."

Joyce does commentaries throughout the *Everyday Life Bible*, and in Deuteronomy she wrote, "Make up your mind that you will not give up until victory is complete and you have taken possession of your rightful inheritance. Do not stay in any one place but keep moving forward toward everything God has for you." By the way, the following April, I was living in a cool little town in the beautiful state of Arizona.

November 1

I asked God to help me find a way to get my life back on track. Then, I decided to go to the gym, where I was reminded that I had set a goal to drop 9.5 pounds and be 190 by November 1. After my workout, I went to weigh myself. Lo and behold, I weighed exactly 190 pounds and that's when it occurred to me that God just revealed the way to get my life back on track. I will do the exact same goal setting process I did to drop 9.5 pounds (preset goals with specific deadlines) and apply the same methodology, but combined with prayer, to every category of my life: spiritual, physical, emotional, financial, relational, and intellectual.

November 2
I decided to take a nap, but right before I did, I asked God to tell me what to do about my final month of rent. I took my Jesus plaque and put it on my chest as I lay down to rest.

Lo and behold, the second I woke up from my twenty-minute nap, the word *roommate* came out of my mouth. I didn't know if this meant for me to get a roommate, or be a roommate, but either way, it was my answer. Within thirty days, I moved in with my best friend.

November 3
Before God chose my new roommate, I'd been praying about clarification on the right woman for me. One of the two women I was dating sent me a text: "Even though I care deeply for you, this will not work." Once again, I received an answered prayer. The woman God chose for me is Joni who gave me the Joyce Meyer *Everyday Life Bible* that helped set off this amazing spiritual experience I've been sharing with you.

November 4
In my journal today, I was writing about the specific *failures* throughout my life and what I did wrong and what I learned. Then, I prayed. *Dear God, give me a clear enough vision to make the correct goals around Your desire for my life. Also, please give me the faith to believe that I can do all things through Jesus Christ who gives me strength. Amen.*

Lo and behold, I got goosebumps all over my body as I read my random Bible opening in Romans where Joyce Meyer in the *Life Point* section of her *Everyday Life Bible* stated: "God did not create us for failure. We may fail at some things on our way to success, but if we trust Him, He will take even our errors and work them out for our own good (See Romans 8:28). God can take our mistakes and turn them into miracles, if we continue to trust confidently in Him." Once again, God met me in the present moment and answered me perfectly.

> We are assured and know that [God being a partner in labor] all things work together and are [fitting into a plan] for good to and for those who love God and are called according to [His] design and purpose. (Romans 8:28)

November 5

In my miracle journal, I was doing some reflecting and remembering how God had spoken simple words of instruction to my heart. For example, when I put my head on the desk and prayed for an answer on how to get a book publisher and I immediately heard, **Turn Around**. And when I did, I was staring at my bookshelf and found my publisher. Within a few weeks I had a book contract with the world's largest publisher of financial books.

Also, I reflected on the time I went to the Deschutes River and prayed and asked God where I should move my family when I heard, **Winthrop**. Next thing I know, within one month's time, my family and I were living in Winthrop, Washington. The following two years proved to be the perfect spot for my family.

And the time I prayed at my office and cried out to God for answers to my problems when I wrote down what I believed was from the Lord; **Love Me. Trust Me. The Truth will set you free. The answers are within you now**. It occurred to me that God speaks to me with simple words. Lo and behold, here is what I read the next morning.

November 6

The next day I prayed and did my random Bible opening and turned exactly to 2 Peter 1:13: "I think it right, as long as I am in this tabernacle, to stir you up by remembrance." This non-random opening was perfectly specific to my final written thought in my miracle-journal the previous day about remembering how God spoke to my heart.

November 7

Eighteen months earlier, my tooth in the back of my mouth cracked and eventually brought me serious pain. Joni and I prayed for the pain to go away, and the very next day it was completely gone. However, on this day, I started to feel some new discomfort in the back of my mouth where my broken tooth resided. I recalled how Jesus healed my pain instantly, and I decided to ignore the small amount of remaining discomfort.

Lo and behold, I felt a crack in my mouth. Then, I spat out a small piece of a broken tooth into my hand, and I noticed the discomfort in my mouth was all gone. I also realized that having this part of my broken tooth out of my mouth relieved the pressure I was feeling in my gums. Could it be God knocked the little piece of tooth out of my mouth to relieve the pain? I believe He did, and I felt no pain until I eventually got a root canal.

November 8

I just finished reading an inspirational chapter in *The Positive Power of Jesus Christ*, by Norman Vincent Peale. I circled the word *power* multiple times on this day. After I prayed, I thought about the word *power*, and I felt God would speak to me in my random Bible opening about it. Lo and behold, I opened exactly to 1 Corinthians 4:20 where I realized that I needed to live at a much higher level to receive more of God's power.

> For the Kingdom of God is not based on talk but on power. (1 Corinthians 4:20 AMP)

November 9

I read from my favorite Christian book of all time; *The life of Christ*, where the word *new* stood out to me. I had a strong feeling that I should read further in Corinthians (the previous day's random Bible opening). Lo and behold, I read in 1 Corinthians 5:7 in my Joyce Meyer *Everyday Life Bible*: "Purge (clean out) the old leaven that you may be fresh (new) dough, still uncontaminated (as you are) for Christ, our Passover (lamb), has been sacrificed."

November 10

This morning I read more from my two favorite books on Jesus Christ in my daily Hour of Spiritual Power. In *The Positive Power of Jesus Christ*, Norman Vincent Peale spoke about how he surrendered his life to Jesus in "success or failure," saying, "Lord, I am fed up with being this way. I don't need to succeed. This is not what I went into the ministry to do. So, I hereby surrender myself fully. If you want me to fail, that is all right with me. I give myself to you to use wherever and in whatever way you desire. If it is to be a failure, so be it." I got on my knees and prayed a similar prayer, but I asked God to continue to give me wisdom even in my failures.

Lo and behold, I randomly opened to 2 Chronicles where I read in *Putting the Word to Work* where Joyce Meyer wrote: "If someone wanted to give you either wealth or wise counsel, which would you choose? Although the riches of Solomon surpassed those of all the kings of earth, it was his wisdom that other rulers sought. Recognize that God-given wisdom is far more valuable than wealth" (2 Chronicles 9:23). And all the kings of the earth sought the presence of Solomon to hear his wisdom, which God had put in his mind.

Once again, God met me in the present moment and answered me powerfully and specifically to my prayer. Here is what I wrote in my miracle-journal; "As I read these words, I was filled with the Holy Spirit and nearly in a state of disbelief. I continue to be blown away, but God is rewarding my total faith and love for Him."

Here is the *Life Point* Joyce made in 2 Chronicles: "Where there is prayer, there is power," and "God wants to display His glory in and through us as dramatically as He did in the physical temple of Solomon's day." This random Bible opening impacted me greatly. I decided to go back to the very front of 2 Chronicles to read where Joyce Meyer introduces Chronicles with these words:

> Just as 1 Chronicles recounts the reign of King David, 2 Chronicles records the rule of David's son, King Solomon, who is often called the wisest man who ever lived." She goes on to say; "one of the ongoing themes of 2 Chronicles is the instruction to seek God. Because of their history, God's people knew how miserable their lives could be when they did not seek Him and how blessed they would be when they did inquire of Him. Nevertheless, God continually reminded them in various ways throughout Chronicles to consult Him in every situation.

Finally, as I read on, I was reminded of my prayer for wisdom, (even in failure) this day.

> Give me wisdom and knowledge to go out and come in before this people, for who can rule this Your people who are so great? God replied to Solomon, Because this was in your heart and you have not asked for riches, possessions, honor, and glory, or the life of your foes, or even for long life, but have asked for wisdom and knowledge for yourself, that you may rule and judge My people over whom I have made you king, wisdom and knowledge are granted you. (2 Chronicles 1:10– 12 AMP)

November 11

I was on fire emotionally and intellectually as I felt God instructed me on inner wisdom. I sat down and did a detailed introspection into myself where God really showed me how I tick. In other words, I received wisdom into who I am. As Socrates said, "Know thyself." I've been praying for wisdom, and apparently God wanted me to start on the inside by recognizing the wisdom I've acquired over fifty years of life. I also recalled in my journal how God had intervened powerfully in my life whenever I reached out to Him in prayer.

November 12

I had just awakened from a twenty-minute nap where the word *goals* was in my dream and on my mind. Also, the word *power* had once again been on my mind where I had just read from Joyce: "Where there is prayer, there is power." Finally, I struggled with my desire to work more enthusiastically. I prayed and asked God to show me the word *goal* in the Bible and to put all these puzzle pieces together in my mind.

Lo and behold, (amazingly enough) I did my random Bible opening to Philippians where I see the words *goals, desire,* and *power* all on one page! Here's what I read on the exact page I opened to in my *Everyday Life Bible* in Philippians 2:12–13:

> Therefore, my dear ones. As you have always obeyed (my suggestions), so now, not only (with enthusiasm you would show) in my presence but much more because I am absent, work out (cultivate, carry out the goal, and fully complete) your own salvation with reverence and awe and trembling (not in your own strength) for it is God Who is all the while effectively at work in you (energizing and creating in you the power and desire), both to will and to do work for His good pleasure and satisfaction and delight.

Can there be any doubt God was up to something in all of this? Even disbelievers must admit there is something bigger going on vs. a long series of coincidences.

God Puts All the Pieces Together

What could all this possibly mean? Here's what I wrote in my miracle-journal:

> When I first asked God for wisdom, I did a random Bible opening to Ecclesiastes where the word wisdom was all over the page and my index finger pointed to Solomon, the wisest man in the Old Testament. I believe God had made it clear in his word that wisdom is much greater than riches. I will continue to acquire wisdom through God's Word. When I combine *goals, power, desire, and wisdom*, I believe God is putting all the pieces into this final puzzle: *Intensely desired goals with wisdom acquired in relation to the goal, and backed by God, will create a goal with unlimited power behind it.*

I continued to write this summation in my journal:

> I believe God is saying to me that I should write goals around the desires He puts on my heart and back my goals with His wisdom and knowledge and put true power behind all of my goals by praying and trusting God to help me accomplish my goals. In other words, the Father, and His spirit in me through Jesus Christ, is the ultimate power to put behind every goal I set. I will now describe my personal goals, backed by the power of God, as Power Goals.

November 13

I decided to fill out my three-ring Dream Goal Binder where I put all my dreams and goals with specific plans and pictures of my rewards. I updated my goals, and now, they reflect my heart's true desire. I went to my desk and prayed to Jesus to bless my Dream Goal Binder by putting His power behind all my goals and to give me the energy to achieve them. I specifically asked Him to put His unlimited power behind all my dreams and goals. Right after I did this, I sat down with my eyes closed and did my random Bible opening.

Lo and behold, I opened once again to Philippians 2:12–13, exactly where I opened the day before! Believe it or not, with my eyes closed, my index finger pointed to the exact same place as well! Not only were the words *goal, power,* and *desire* on the page but so was *energy* on that very page.

Also, here's what Joyce Meyer's *Life Point* message was on the same exact page I randomly opened to: "Yet, this passage (Philippians 2:5) clearly exhorts us to be of the same humble mind that Jesus displayed; to think of others and to be more concerned for their interests and welfare than our own, and to do nothing from conceit or empty arrogance. If we are obedient to this instruction, if we humble ourselves and are willing to serve others, we will live in harmony and therefore be pleasing to God." Let this same attitude and purpose and (humble) mind be in you which was in Christ Jesus.

November 14

In my miracle journal I wrote, "Wow! God keeps blowing my mind." I was sitting in my recliner and doing my Hour of Spiritual Power, and a thought impacted my mind, so I wrote the imparted idea in my miracle notebook: "Birds of the air, lilies of the field—God has provided, and God will provide." I immediately felt a strong urge to pray: *God were these words from you?* I then grabbed my Jesus plaque, and with my eyes closed, I prayed as I did my random Bible opening. Lo and behold, I opened exactly to Hebrews 4:16:

Let us then fearlessly and confidently and boldly draw near to the throne of Grace and find Grace to help in good time for every need (appropriate help and well-timed help, coming just when we need it).

Joyce Meyer furthers the point by saying: "You can rest in God because you know he will take care of you and meet your needs."

Amazing! I just wrote, "God will provide for all my needs" in my miracle journal and immediately did a random Bible opening during a sincere prayer. Once again God met me in the present moment. In a very real way these were all instant miracles having God speak directly to my heart in a two-way form of communication. I understand all the supernatural experiences I've written in this book as answered prayers, supernatural events, and instant miracles. After each time I said a sincere prayer and made my request, I fully expected God would meet my need in the present moment, and He always did.

November 15
I listed in my journal some other wonderful things God did for me and some future miracles I desired in my life. One miracle request looks like a near impossibility and that's the repair of the broken relationship with my two daughters after their mom and I divorced. It will take time for this seemingly improbable miracle to manifest but I believe "with God all things are possible," and I believe in God's perfect timing. This prayed-for miracle looks unlikely, but over time, one year or ten years, this seemingly impossible miracle will become a reality. God will deliver again.

November 16
On this day I reflected on the incredible experiences of the previous several weeks. Here's what I wrote: "God is doing a very good thing for me. He sees through my weaknesses and failures and goes directly to my heart. I asked God for answers with a believing heart, and He is delivering in spades."

November 17

The next morning, in my Hour of Spiritual Power, I did a journal entry about living in joy, and I used the word *finish*. In fact, *finish* was the last word I wrote. I decided to close my eyes and pray. I asked God to speak to me about what I just wrote in my journal. I then did my random Bible opening with my eyes closed and let God direct me on where to open the Bible. Lo and behold, (incredibly enough) I opened directly to Acts where my eyes went right to Acts 20:24: "if only I may finish my course with joy."

As you can imagine I was absolutely blown away and immediately I felt the Holy Spirit come upon me after reading those confirming words. I knew that message was from God and for me. In my heart, I felt like God was saying I must finish this book, and I must finish what I start, and equally important, I must start and finish each day with joy. In summary, we should always *finish* what we start and do everything with joy in our hearts.

> But none of these things move me; neither do I esteem my life dear to myself, if only I may finish my course with joy and the ministry which I have obtained from [which was entrusted to me by] the Lord Jesus, faithfully to attest to the good news (Gospel) of God's grace. (Acts 20:24 AMP)

November 18

I was reading my two books on Jesus: *The Positive Power of Jesus Christ*, by Norman Vincent Peale, and *The Life of Christ*, by Fulton J. Sheen. Norman writes simply as he beautifully describes the power of Jesus Christ in a series of impactful short stories. Fulton writes in a more serious and sophisticated manner as he tells the full story of the Lord in a way I've never read before. On this day, both books highlighted specifically about the incredible power Jesus Christ displayed in His life.

I journaled about deepening my faith in Jesus Christ through a *knowing*: "I will deepen my faith in Jesus so when it's my time to leave this earth, I will go out with the highest level of security about heaven because of my relationship with God. I will go in peace *knowing* (having a knowing)." Then, I prayed: *God, give me your thoughts on all that's happened in the last couple weeks of your wisdom given to me in my Bible openings.* Lo and behold, I opened exactly to 2 Timothy 3:14–15:

> But as for you, continue to hold to the things that you have learned and of which you are convinced, knowing from which you learned them ... in absolute trust and confidence in His power, wisdom, and goodness.

Amazing! As you can imagine, I was blown away because once again, God met me in the present moment. For me, this was yet more evidence that Jesus can answer prayers, even instantly. When I first set out to prove God could perform instant miracles in my life, I had no idea what that would mean or how He would manifest them in my life. I believed He would perform miracles, and I believed like that of a child.

Lo and behold, I have documented everything as it happened and I'm sharing them with you in this book. I cataloged it all on little yellow sticky notes in my Joyce Meyer *Everyday Life Bible* along with specific dates, and everything was noted in my miracle journals. To my own satisfaction, God has proved that if a person sincerely asks in prayer and truly believes with all his heart, mind, and soul for that which is asked, Jesus will listen, and God will deliver. The powerful formula from the Lord: ask, believe, and receive.

Later that evening after the excitement wore off from my random opening on "knowing," I wrote this in my journal:

> The Lord said it when He walked the earth that He wants to give us what we desire. But there's a catch. We must have deep belief with 100% faith

and trust in God and ask with a pure heart. If only we could believe with all our hearts ... if only we could pray with no doubts ... if only we could trust God's answers in His perfect timing, then, and only then, within reason, we can receive what we ask for in prayer.

November 19

Lo and behold, the very next morning, with my eyes closed (as usual), I randomly opened my Bible to First Timothy, where my eyes went directly to First Timothy 1:5 (AMP):

> Whereas the object and purpose of our instruction and charge is love, which springs from a pure heart, and a good conscience, and sincere faith.

As the night wore on, I had four candles going with the lights off in my apartment, and I prayed: *Jesus, give me a clear vision of my future, the future You desire for my life. Amen.* Lo and behold, about five minutes later, as I was reclined in my chair with my eyes closed, I had a clear vision come to the forefront of my mind! It was me speaking to a fairly large audience. After I saw this vision, it was obvious that Jesus had something in mind that didn't seem likely to me. However, I knew I must be on high alert for more clarity where this vision from the Lord is concerned.

Mark my words when I tell you this; Jesus met me in that moment only five minutes after I prayed. He met me in the present moment by answering specifically to what I had just prayed. And even though the answer didn't seem likely to me at that moment I received the vision, I knew it was from Him and that His Will for my life will eventually come to fruition. Over time, I'm confident that the Lord will help me fill in the blanks.

Later that evening, I had a text exchange with Joni about the vision. In the series of texts that went back and forth, the word *messenger* was brought up. I sent her this exact text: "I'm a mess, not a messenger." I sent this text because at that time of my life, my financial situation was an absolute mess. In other words, how could someone like me be a messenger for God when my life was in such a mess? I'm disappointed in myself to have texted that statement since God had literally poured out His spiritual blessings right along with blessing me physically, emotionally, relationally, and intellectually.

November 20

Lo and behold, on the next morning's random Bible opening, the very first paragraph I opened in my Joyce Meyer *Everyday Life Bible* were these exact words:

> Paul, an apostle (special messenger) of Christ Jesus by appointment and command of God our savior and of Christ Jesus (the Messiah), our hope. (1 Timothy 1:1 AMP)

I immediately thought to myself, *This is absolutely incredible!* as I pondered what all these random Bible openings could possibly mean. So, I prayed intensely, and as I did, these three words were spoken to my mind: **Empower My people**. I can tell you there was no doubt this was a direct command from God. I immediately wrote in my journal about those words imprinted into my mind and prayed again: *God, please confirm these words imprinted upon my mind were from You.*

Lo and behold, my random Bible opening took me exactly to 1 Thessalonian 5:19–21 where God answered my question in prayer perfectly.

> Do not quench (suppress or subdue) the [Holy] Spirit; Do not spurn the gifts and utterances of the prophets [do not depreciate prophetic revelations nor despise inspired instruction or exhortation or

warning]. But test and prove all things [until you can recognize] what is good; [to that] hold fast. (1 Thessalonians 5:19–21 AMP)

Once I finished reading Thessalonians, I received further confirmation as my entire being was filled with the incredible power of the Holy Spirit. I immediately prayed again and thanked God for this perfectly answered prayer and instant miracle. Honestly, could God have had me open the Bible to a better place than this?

As you can imagine, God had my full attention. I felt overwhelmed by what was happening, as this was way out of my league of understanding. Yet, for some reason, God was not only speaking to my heart, mind, and soul, but he was meeting me in the present moment with perfect answers to my specific prayers.

Joyce Meyer goes on to clarify a prophet to that of prophecy. She says in her *Life Point,* "There are, of course, modern day prophets gifted by God to foretell future events, but not everyone who prophesies is called to stand in the office of a prophet. First Corinthians 12:10 states that prophecy is the gift of interpreting the divine will and purpose of God." She continues, "The Amplified Bible says, not to depreciate prophetic revelations. In both the Old Testament and New Testament, prophets were valuable vessels for God. In the Old Testament, God spoke to His people using prophets as His mouthpieces."

November 24
Here is what I wrote on this day in my miracle journal: "I continue to be blown away—I'm not sure exactly how this is happening, but it happened yet again! I was writing on my index cards about *finishing.* In fact, it was the very last word I wrote. I then put the card down and said a sincere prayer. I intentionally opened the Bible super-fast, almost as if I were trying to dismiss all that's happened in these 'random' Bible openings."

Lo and behold, I randomly opened my Joyce Meyer *Everyday Life Bible* to these exact words: "God will finish the work." The word *finish* was all over the page and in fact appeared seven more times! By the end, Joyce Meyer says, "God has promised to finish the work He's started in you. Will you make a similar commitment to Him to finish whatever He gives you to do in this life?" It was right here that I wept as the Holy Spirit covered me from head to toe and confirmed what just happened and had been happening.

I continued to write in my journal: "I feel God wants me to finish this book. I also believe He wants me to finish this 'thing' we have been doing together. In other words, God has shown me that His power is for real and it's available right now. God will answer prayers and He will perform miracles, even instant ones."

I can't fully explain how all this impacted me, but I knew that even though I could not see God, I felt His presence throughout this entire journey. God is an invisible spirit, and He works in mysterious ways. Think of God like the wind. You can't see the wind, but you experience it nonetheless, so you know it exists. I already knew God existed because of the many amazing miracles He had already performed upon my behalf. For myself, there is simply no other explanation for all these supernatural events except that God hears our prayers, and He and His Son fulfill promises by way of miracles, signs, and wonders.

In summary, I experienced God, like I experienced the wind before a storm is about to hit. The past several weeks of non-random Bible openings were not just mere wind. It was God's power that absolutely blew me away. His demonstrated power had multiple times brought me to my knees in awe of Him. I believe God responded the way He did because I prayed with a sincere heart and had no doubt that He would provide me with direct answers. I reached out to the Lord with all my heart, mind, and soul, and He answered and many times He answered instantly. I compared the wind to God, but God, through His Son Jesus Christ, turned the wind of the Holy Spirit into a hurricane of fulfilled promises for me.

CHAPTER SEVEN

God Is with Us

Have not I commanded thee? Be strong and of good courage; be not afraid, neither be thou dismayed: for the Lord thy God is with thee whithersoever thou goest.

—Joshua 1:9 KJV

As you might imagine, after weeks of supernatural answers from God, I was in a heightened state of spiritual awareness. The consecutive string of perfect answers on my random Bible openings had me in total awe of the Lord. These spiritual manifestations took me into another dimension of mind. It seemed to me that divine intervention happened each day at the soul level of my very being. It's indescribable to articulate what I was experiencing and feeling inside. I was living in the spiritual realm of the universe.

At the end of November, when I finished reviewing the supernatural events that I recorded in my miracle journal, I was in a state of bewilderment about all that happened. I decided to go for a hike in the woods. It was a beautiful sunny day in Bend, Oregon, where fresh snow was melting. The sky was a pristine blue, and everything outside seemed to sparkle from the reflection off the snow from the sun. It was the kind of day you feel blessed to be alive. I headed down the hill toward the Deschutes River trail. At the very bottom, I decided to go off the beaten path and walked straight into the middle of the forest.

As I hiked deep into the woods, I prayed to God to help me listen to anything he had to say. A couple minutes later, I was powerfully impressed with these words: **It is time to go on a new path.** In my heart I knew God was referring to the future direction of my life. Only a few seconds later I heard: **Follow Me. Follow My ways.** As I continued my hike, I also heard: **Place your trust in Me. I can move mountains.** I believe God said to my heart that He could remove the mountain of problems I was facing.

As I hiked further into the forest, I had a penetrating thought that this book was going to find its way into many hands. I had a strong feeling that it would lead to many people finding God's power and doing incredible things in the name of His Son—Jesus Christ. Suddenly, I noticed a jet plane far away in the clouds tearing through the sky. At that exact moment, these words were impressed upon my heart and mind: **Greater things than this you will see. All things are possible through Me.** A high-speed jet soaring through the sky was a well-timed sight, but I knew God was going to show me something much more powerful. At the end of this book, you will read about the greater things that God showed me.

As I crunched through the thick, icy snow, I heard: **Stop pushing. Trust Me. I can move heaven and earth in front of you.** I looked up at the beautiful, frosted trees and heard these words in my heart, mind, and soul: **Follow your new path.** Then, I prayed and asked: *Is that You, God? Has it been You showing me these miraculous signs and wonders?* Immediately, my entire being was intensely overwhelmed with the power of the Holy Spirit, which was clear confirmation that the answer was **Yes!**

When I was alone in the middle of the Deschutes National Forest, I felt like Jesus was right there walking with me. In the exact moment of sensing His mighty presence, I started to shed tears of joy. I then felt guided to walk about fifteen yards in a different direction toward a particular pine tree. Honestly, it didn't look different than any other tree. As I stood below it, I looked up to the top where melted ice fell upon my face in what looked like teardrops falling from the sky. In that moment it felt like God picked this particular tree to mix His sparkling raindrops with my tears of joy.

As I stood deep in the forest, under the tree, I heard that inner voice from God say to me: **Retrace your steps.** God likely wanted me to retrace my steps again to really learn from my past choices. I stood there in total peace embraced by the deep silence of nature as God's created beauty surrounded me. Suddenly, I looked down and saw my shadow as the sun gleamed against my back, and I heard the Lord say: **Although you are a mere shadow of Me, you were made in My image.**

As I started to walk through the woods in the ice and snow, I heard: **It will be a difficult uphill climb. I will be with you every step of the way.** As I started to walk down the mountain, I immediately had this strong impression from God that I was supposed to send this book (once completed) to Joel Osteen.

Lo and behold, within five seconds of that specific thought, my cell phone alerted me that a text message just arrived. I looked down at my phone, and believe it or not, there was a text from Joni sending me a picture of Joel Osteen with a Bible quote underneath his photo! I was left in total awe of the power of God and His perfect timing. I believe that God supernaturally imprinted Joel Osteen into my mind right before Joni's text to confirm that I was in fact surrounded by His presence.

God Instructs

I sought the Lord, and He heard me, and delivered me from all my fears. (Psalm 34:4 NKJV)

For the next several days, I read everything I noted in my miracle journal, which included what I wrote after obeying the command:

"Retrace your steps." When I looked over the entire course of my life, I felt extremely sad. I worked extremely hard to provide a good life for my family. I set and achieved many exciting goals along the way, but in the end, I felt like it was all for nothing. In fact, I felt like Job in the Bible. Let me explain.

Over the course of fifteen years, I had many successes that ultimately ended with me going broke multiple times. In fact, for a short period of time, I was nearly homeless, meaning I had no money or job, and I was living with family or friends. At one point, I lost my mental health by going into a deep depression. At another point, I lost my physical health and lived with debilitating stomach pain.

It gets worse. I had two cars repossessed, and the most recent business failure had left me with $1 million in debt. To make matters even worse, in the divorce, I lost my relationships with my two precious daughters. To top it all off, I lost friendships along the way, and I lost my reputation in the process of everything that happened in both my professional and personal life.

In summary, over the course of the last fifteen years; I lost my physical health, my mental health, followed by my financial health, and finally, I lost my family in the divorce and lost the wonderful relationship I had with my two daughters that I loved with all my heart. But through it all, I never blamed God, and in fact, I always turned to Him for comfort.

December 6: Here's what I wrote in my miracle journal: "It was all for nothing. All my years of hard work and trying to do the right things, which included being a great dad, was worthless because it resulted in nothing. I have no possessions and even if I did, so what. My daughters don't seem to appreciate how hard I worked to provide them with a wonderful childhood. The sacrifices I had to make for the entire family along the way for our very survival, meaningless in their eyes. I have no relationship with them, and it's been three years running. I was tossed aside like a worthless piece of garbage."

After writing all of this, I became very emotional. I decided to go to Ashland, Oregon, to one of my favorite hiking spots called Grizzly Peak. Before I went, I asked Joni where it was exactly in the Bible that King Solomon had a similar revelation about his life. She directed me to Ecclesiastes.

> And whatever my eyes desired I kept not from them; I withheld not my heart from any pleasure, for my heart rejoiced in all my labor, and this was my portion and reward for all my toil. (Ecclesiastes 2:10 AMP)

> Then I looked on all that my hands had done and the labor I had spent in doing it, and behold, all was vanity and a striving after the wind and a feeding on it, and there was no profit under the sun. (2:11)

> The wise man's eyes are in his head, but the fool walks in darkness; and yet I perceived that [in the end] one event happens to them both. (2:14)

> Then said I in my heart, As it happens to the fool, so it will happen even to me. And of what use is it then for me to be more wise? Then I said in my heart, This is also vanity! (2:15)

> For the wise man, the same as the fool, there is no remembrance, since in the days to come all will be long forgotten. And how does the wise man die? Even as the fool! (2:16)

> So I hated life, because what is done under the sun was grievous to me, for all is vanity and a striving after the wind and feeding on it. (2:17)

And I hated all my labor in which I had toiled under
the sun, seeing that I must leave it to the man who
will succeed me. (2:18)

There you have it. As it was for Solomon-the-wise around 930
BC, so it was with me, the fool, on December 6, 2014. With tears
rolling down my cheeks, I drove to my favorite hiking spot in
Southern Oregon. As I started my two-hour hike at Grizzly Peak, I
felt much better. As I hiked and prayed, I asked God to help me in
my time of sorrow.

Lo and behold, God opened my eyes like never before to a part
of the hike where all the trees were black from a massive forest fire.
I heard God say to my heart, **Burn it down! Burn the past down!
Put your past to the flames for a restored heart.**

As I walked a little farther, two trees were in the way of my path.
One was burnt black, but the other had its bright yellow purity left
inside the hollowed-out wood. God said these words to me: **Keep
your heart pure even as others cut you down.** As I arrived at the
top of the mountain, it felt like everything opened up on the inside
of me as the landscape also opened up for me.

On the way down, there was a covering of trees where the mud
was wet when I heard the Lord say: **You will slip along the way.
Stay on your new path.** Then, I decided to veer off the path to see
where a side trail would take me when I heard: **You will take side
roads along the way. Stay on your new path.**

Upon completing the hike, several things became clear to me.
I realized that I toiled in my life for nothing; zero return in every
category except one; my spirituality. It also became clear that in the
remainder of my life I must put God as my number one priority. It
also dawned on me that God is always available, and it was easiest
to feel His presence and hear His voice when I was in nature. Here's
why I believe this is true:

Nature is beautiful as God is beautiful, and God created all
of life's beauty. And where there's beauty, there's love, and where

there is love, God is there too. And where there is greatness of any kind, God is there. Whenever you see love or feel love, wherever you see beauty or experience beauty, or wherever you see greatness or experience greatness, God is there. When you feel touched, whether in joy or sorrow, God is there. God is great, God is love, and God is available when we invite Him inside of our hearts.

I suggest that you start by fully appreciating all the gifts God has bestowed upon you already. Your eyes, ears, hands, feet, and your brain were not acquired by you. They were all given to you by God as He created everything. Just say a deeply sincere prayer of thankfulness, and you will experience "the peace that transcends all understanding."

In the end, if you don't know God, all your efforts will be like "chasing after the wind" because in the end, your labor will count for nothing. Your homes, cars, jewelry, and money will all wither, rust, and die. Family or friends can't fully comfort you in the very end, but they will try their best. No, it will be God's love to comfort you, all the way to the end—your end—when you will need Him the most. You will know Him because you developed a relationship with His Son—Jesus Christ. Not only will this be a relationship to comfort you in the very end of your life but also in the remaining days of your life.

In the very end, you will take only one thing with you that has any meaningful value, and this is your soul. In death, this essential part of you is called your spirit, which is the very essence of you. Your soul stays strong even as you break down in old age and until death when your spirit finally enters eternity. For those who recognize Jesus Christ as their Lord and Savior, this wonderful part of you, the essential-you, will go back to God.

Choose life, by living for God, as nothing else truly matters, especially in the very end of your life. People will desert you, disappoint you, and hurt you. But even if that doesn't happen, in the end, you will leave the ones you love as you pass from this earth. Everything and everyone must die; that's just a fact of life. But lo and behold, in the very end, the essential part of you, your spirit, your soul, will go back to God. However, Jesus told His disciples there are two specific conditions that must be met. First, you must believe in God. Next, you must believe in Jesus Christ because "God's only begotten Son" leaves you with no other choice. In a heartfelt prayer recognize the Messiah, the King of Kings, as your Lord and Savior Who saved the world from sin.

In summary, thank the Lord for dying for your sins by hanging on His cross. Thank Him for displaying the most awesome events in world history: His prediction of His death, His resurrection from the dead on the third day, and His ascension into heaven. Once you do that, then all your sins will be blotted out from God's eyes where He can see you with a cleansed soul. Most assuredly, your soul will be saved, and you will experience the greatest power in heaven and on earth: God and His only begotten Son, Jesus Christ.

CHAPTER EIGHT

God Is Outrageous

And the whole multitude were seeking to touch Him, for power went out from Him and healed them all.

—Luke 6:19 NKJV

As I look back on the mysterious events in my life, one thing stands out. The second I prayed with a believing heart was the moment that I believe Jesus set the miracle in motion. Some of the miracles happened instantly while others took days, weeks, and even months to manifest. My most desired prayer took eight years to be answered, and that outrageous God story makes up the final chapter of this book. It is not for me to ask why all these unexplainable experiences happened because God is a mystery.

In this chapter I will highlight my favorite random Bible openings. Stay with me as all this eventually leads to the most outrageous miracles of my life as the book writing part of my God adventure came to a spectacular ending. For example, God performed two amazing miracles while answering my longest held prayers that completes this book.

Let's look at Webster's definition of the word *outrageous* to better understand exactly what I mean: "Extremely unusual or unconventional; extraordinary and being beyond all reason." Okay, here we go with some more God stories around my random Bible openings where God continued to show me His awesome power.

In January 2015, I started a new miracle notebook titled "Wisdom from the Bible." Inside, the new miracle-notebook started off with the words; "My 2015 walk with God."

January 9

I watched a Joel Osteen sermon titled *Faith is the currency of heaven*: "Your checking account might be low and your business slow, but faith is the key. Think, talk, and act like you're blessed. Smile and hold your head up high. You need to do your part to get your victory. God has already empowered you to do so. He has already blessed you with favor; go and take possession of what God promised you. Start believing you are one of a kind. This is your time, your moment. He has spoken promises to you. You may not have the contacts or the dream, but God has them. God has blessings for those who love the Lord."

Joel thunders: "Believe you can become all God wants you to be. Be bold! Choose to believe that God has called you to be prosperous. Repeat to yourself: I am healthy. I am blessed. I am prosperous. Say it; I am healed, I am restored. I am a masterpiece and add Amen to that! Blessings have their name on them right now just waiting for you to claim. Thank God in advance by saying; thank you God for bringing my dreams to reality." He then quoted Luke 12:32: "For it is your Father's good pleasure to give you the Kingdom."

He continued; "Believe big, as God put a dream in your heart. Enlarge your vision. He created you in His own image. His DNA is on your inside. You are royalty. Stir up your faith by declaring God's favor. Believe new doors will open. The Angels in heaven will go to work when you believe all things are possible. Faith is the currency of heaven."

Then Joel poured it on: "God can rain down blessings. Just believe in what He promises, and God will make it happen. Faith results in an exchange for God's goodness. God is longing to be good to you. As Jesus said, *according to your faith, be it done unto you.* God works by faith. God is with you and all things are possible for your dreams to come true. God will give you the desires of your heart. God will vindicate you."

God Rains Down Blessings

I decided to drive to a beautiful cemetery in Jacksonville, Oregon. As I glanced over the tombstones, I gained a better perspective on my life. There's a particular spot next to a cemetery plot that has a bench with a pretty view. I sat on the bench to think and pray. It was a partially cloudy day, but it was not raining. The sun occasionally peaked through the scattered clouds. I had my Jesus journal with me as I was praying. After my prayer, I felt instructed to do a random Bible opening in the miracle notebook. Lo and behold, I opened to the part of the journal where Joel said; "God can rain down blessings," and at that very moment, one wee drop of rain fell on the word **rain**. This confirmed to me that God will continue to rain down His blessings upon my life.

Then, I looked at the next sentence of my notes where Joel said, "God will make it happen." Lo and behold, it rained another tiny drop on the word **will** and then a tiny drop on the word **happen.** This further confirmed to me that God will make new blessings for my life happen. Then, I glanced down on where Joel said, "God is longing to be good to you." Lo and behold, the raindrop splattered across **good to you.** This last raindrop splatter was perfect confirmation that God is indeed longing to be good to me.

In the exact moment of the last raindrop, the Holy Spirit erupted inside of me. I felt God's presence surrounding me as I looked at the sky. Lo and behold, the sky was opening up in front of my eyes as the clouds departed, and the sun radiated powerfully from behind the clouds. As the sun's rays beamed upon my face, I felt the warmth of God's love cover me. This amazingly powerful experience kept me on the bench for several minutes beaming with immense joy.

Favorite Journal Entries

January 12

This morning, I was reading about justice; specifically, the story of when Jesus visited Simon at his home. Simon was a Pharisee, and he didn't want to compromise himself in the eyes of his fellow Pharisees, most of whom despised Jesus. Simon intentionally omitted all the ordinary courtesies that would have been paid to any other honored guest. I prayed specifically about justice where I asked God to help me to do the right things in life. Lo and behold, my random Bible opening in the *Everyday Life Bible* where my eyes look directly at Isaiah 56:1

> Thus says the Lord: Keep justice, do *and* use righteousness (conformity to the will of God which brings salvation), for My salvation is soon to come, and My righteousness (My rightness and justice) to be revealed.

January 17

I bought a brand-new spiral notebook to write all my goals in the present tense. Brian Tracy suggested doing this in his book titled *No Excuses!* I wrote, "I will become spiritually enlightened by acquiring wisdom from reading God's Word daily." I then prayed about all my present tense goals I had just written in my notebook. After that, I tossed the Bible all around in different directions in my hands before doing my random Bible opening.

Lo and behold, (believe it or not) my eyes go directly to Joyce Meyer *Putting the Word to Work*: "Receiving good teaching from pastors, teachers, and ministers is a blessing, but it is equally important to study Scripture for yourself (see Acts 17:10, 11). Do you regularly set aside time each day to read the Word of God? If not, ask him to help you have a hunger to read and study His Word, and make every effort to do so daily."

> Now the brethren at once sent Paul and Silas by night to Berea and when they arrived, they entered the synagogue of the Jews. Now these [Jews] were better disposed and more noble than those in Thessalonica, for they were entirely ready and accepted and welcomed the message [concerning the attainment through Christ of eternal salvation in the kingdom of God] with inclination of mind and eagerness, searching and examining the Scriptures daily to see if these things were so. (Acts 17:10–11 AMP)

January 27

I just finished reading about the Transfiguration of Jesus in my *Life of Christ* book. I would like to share with you some of what Fulton J. Sheen wrote on the Transfiguration: "Three important scenes of our Lord's life took place on Mountains. On one He preached the Beatitudes, the practice of which would bring a cross from the world; on the second, He showed the glory that lay beyond the cross; and on the third, He offered Himself in death as a prelude to His glory and that of all who would believe in His name."

He continues, "The second incident took place within a few weeks, at most, of Calvary, when he took with Him to a high mountain; Peter, James, and John; Peter the rock, James destined to be the first Apostle-martyr; and John the visionary of the future glory of the Apocalypse. These three were present when He raised from the dead the daughter of Jairus. All three needed to learn the lesson of the cross and to rectify their false perceptions of the

Messiah. Peter had vehemently protested the cross, while James and John had been throne-seekers. To believe in His Calvary, they must see the glory that shone beyond the scandal of the cross.

"On the mountaintop, after praying, He became transfigured before them as the glory of His divinity flashed through the threads of His earthly raiment. It was not so much a light that was shining from without as the beauty of the Godhead that shone from within."

"As the Cross came nearer, His glory became greater. In man, the body is a kind of a cage of the soul. In Christ, the body was the Temple of Divinity. Here in the Transfiguration, the divinity shone through humanity. It took restraint to hide the divinity that was in Him."

> And even as He prayed, the fashion of His face was altered, and His garments became white and dazzling; and two men appeared conversing with Him, Moses, and Elias, seen now in glory; and they spoke of the death which He was to achieve at Jerusalem. (Luke 9:30–31)

After reading all of this from the *Life of Christ*, I prayed and asked God to show me something about what I had just read regarding Peter, James, and John. As I went to do my random Bible opening, the Bible fell out of my hands and landed, fully opened, on the table in front of me. I knew the *Everyday Life Bible* had just opened to exactly where God wanted me to read. Lo and behold, the Bible mysteriously opened to 1 Peter 5:6: "Therefore humble yourselves [demote, lower yourselves in your own estimation] under the mighty hand of God, that in due time He may exalt you."

January 26

Lo and behold, just a few days after my prayer for vision, I watched a Joyce Meyer video and here's what she said: "Know the dream you're going after each day. Keep your vision in front of you always." She quoted Proverbs and Habakkuk:

Without vision the people perish. (Proverbs 29:18 AMP)

And the Lord answered me and said, write the vision and engrave it so plainly upon tablets that everyone who passes may read as he hastens by. (Habakkuk 2:2 AMP)

Lo and behold, after a prayer, I decided to do my random opening in my new miracle-journal where I opened precisely to these words about writing goals for clearer vision in my life: "Power Goals: Put God's power behind all goals through the power of prayer. God can help me achieve my spiritual goals and sometimes instantly, but always miraculously."

January 27
On this day I prayed specifically to God: *Please advise me on life and on my work*. Lo and behold, my random Bible opening had my eyes land on Exodus 31:14–15:

> You shall keep the Sabbath for it is holy to you ...
> six days may work be done, but the seventh is the
> Sabbath of rest, sacred to the Lord.

January 28
I just finished reading again about justice, wisdom, and spiritual enlightenment in my Dream Goal Miracle Binder. I prayed specifically to God: *Please speak to me about wisdom and justice*. Lo and behold, my random Bible opening in the Joyce Meyer *Everyday Life Bible*, went directly to Job 33:26, where the words *justice, wisdom* and *enlightenment* were all revealed!

> He prays to God, and He is favorable to him, so that
> he sees His face with joy; for [God] restores to him
> his righteousness [his uprightness and right standing

with God—with its joys]. He looks upon other men or sings out to them, I have sinned and perverted that which was right, and it did not profit me, or He did not requite me [according to my iniquity]! [God] has redeemed my life from going down to the pit [of destruction] and my life shall see the light! [Elihu comments] Behold, God does all things twice, yes, three times, with a man. To bring back his life from the pit [of destruction], that he may be enlightened with the light of the living. Give heed, O Job, listen to me; hold your peace, and I will speak. If you have anything to say, answer me; speak, for I desire to justify you. If [you do] not [have anything to say], listen to me; hold your peace, and I will teach you wisdom. (Job 33:26–33 AMP)

January 31

I bought a new book titled *The Wisdom of God*, by Nancy Guthrie. I had just finished page 96 where I read Psalm 1:1: "Blessed is the man who walks not in the counsel of the wicked, nor stands in the way of sinners, nor sits in the seat of scoffers." After reading these words, I immediately prayed for new blessings in my life before doing a Bible opening. Lo and behold, my random Bible opening went directly to Deuteronomy 28 where I read the word *BLESS, Blessed, and Blessing* nineteen times in just a couple pages!

If you will listen diligently to the voice of the Lord your God, being watchful to do all His commandments which I command you this day, the Lord your God will set you high above all the nations on the earth.

And all these blessings shall come upon you and overtake you if you heed the voice of the Lord your God.

Blessed shall you be in the city and blessed shall you be in the field.

Blessed shall be the fruit of your body and the fruit of your ground and the fruit of your beasts, the increase of your cattle and the young of your flock.

Blessed shall your basket and your kneading trough.

Blessed shall you be when you come in and blessed shall you be when you go out. (Deuteronomy 28:1–6 AMP)

The word *blessing* continues. On the very same page, here's the *Life Point* where Joyce Meyer says: "God showers blessings on those who decide to live wholeheartedly for him and make obedience to him in their lifestyle." On the very next page Joyce uses the word *blessing* ten more times under the title "Receiving Outrageous Blessings."

July 16: As I was typing this chapter, God did something *outrageous* for me. It would be logical to assume God would perform some unexplainable events, or what I call miracles, while I was writing this book. On this morning something interesting happened. I woke up at 4:40 a.m., made a cup of coffee, and went outside to pray. After I prayed, I had this strong feeling God wanted to show me something at the pool. I quickly finished my coffee, put on my bathing suit, and headed for a swim.

After taking a quick hot tub, I jumped in the pool. I started swimming with my eyes closed in a fully relaxed state as I prayed specifically for Joni, who had some health issues. When I opened my eyes, I noticed a tiny butterfly trapped in the pool. I softly lifted the water underneath him to rescue the tiny butterfly from drowning. As I did, he flew like a rocket ship out of the water until he was quickly out of sight.

I did a couple more laps, and then I came back to the exact same spot and there he was in the corner of the pool. Once again, I picked up the tiny butterfly slowly with some water underneath him. As the water quickly drained through my fingers, he stayed in my hand. I immediately recognized what was going on. I knew in that very instant this little guy wasn't going anywhere. I was so confident he was going to sit in my hand that I took him to the hot tub with me with my left hand up in the air away from the hot water. Then, I had this feeling he was supposed to go back to my apartment, which was about seventy yards away from the pool. I dried off and packed my gym bag with my right hand. I had little concern that the tiny butterfly was going to leave my left hand.

When I returned to the apartment, something wild happened. I held the little creature high above my head in my left hand. Then, for the first time, I did all I could to not disturb him. I looked at him high above me in my left hand, and then I proceeded to look down as I dumped my gym bag of clothes out on the couch below me with my right hand.

Lo and behold, the tiny butterfly emerged up from underneath the bottom of my clothes! I looked up at my left hand thinking it must have been a different butterfly, but it was the same one! As if by magic, he disappeared from my left hand far above my head and emerged from underneath my clothes on the couch. This was done only a second after I had just seen him far above my head where he was sitting in my left hand. I was mystified, but immediately I knew God was giving me a new story for this book.

The tiny butterfly proceeded to fly to the window because he wanted to be outside. I carefully caught him in a tiny container and brought him outside on the balcony where I placed him. I was going to get Joni and show her, but I thought better of it because she was getting ready for work. One hour later, I went outside to see if he was still there. Interestingly, he was. About ten minutes later, before Joni headed off to work, I asked her to look at him. After glancing at him carefully she asked; "Is he dead?" At that very moment, he suddenly flew off the balcony.

As we walked inside, Joni asked me what it all meant. I told her that earlier I had a strong impression that God had something to show me at the pool. About twenty minutes later, I sent Joni the following text: "I think the little butterfly was a confirmation that God heard my deep prayer for you this morning." About fifteen seconds after I sent that text, I opened the Bible to where I left off the previous day, and I saw the word *hear* twelve times in 1 Kings 8. This is where King Solomon stood in the court before the Lord's altar in the presence of all the assembly of Israel and spread forth his hands toward heaven in prayer.

> But will God indeed dwell with men on the earth? Behold the heavens and heaven of heavens [in its most extended compass] cannot contain You; how much less this house I have built?
>
> Yet graciously consider the prayer and supplication of Your servant, O Lord my God, to hearken to the [loud] cry and prayer which he prays before You today,
>
> That Your eyes may be open toward this house night and day, toward the place of which You have said, My Name [and the token of My presence] shall be there, that You may hearken to the prayer which Your servant shall make in [or facing toward] this place.
>
> Hearken to the prayer of Your servant and of Your people Israel when they pray in *or* toward this place. Hear in heaven Your dwelling place, and when You hear, forgive. (1 Kings 8:27–30 AMP)

For me, the random Bible opening, and the magic butterfly were clear confirmation that God heard my prayer. Right after I finished reading 1 Kings 8, I told Joni the story and had her read 1 Kings 8 to support my belief that God heard my prayer for her that day in the pool.

In summary, God performed new supernatural events as I was typing this chapter of the book. As I was journaling about the magic butterfly in my journal, I thought to myself, *Why wouldn't God do something outrageous as I was in the middle of writing this book about miracles and the power of prayer?* Well, of course He would, and of course He did. I closed this chapter with great anticipation of other supernatural surprises God had in store for me.

CHAPTER NINE

God Is Mysterious

Jesus said unto him, If thou canst believe, all things are possible to him that believeth.

—Mark 9:23 KJV

I Googled multiple definitions of the word *mysterious*, and here's the one I liked best: "difficult or impossible to understand, explain, or identify." The many miracles that happened to me over the years would certainly fall under this definition of mysterious. Here's another definition on the internet: *puzzling, strange, peculiar, curious, funny, odd, bizarre, mystifying, inexplicable, baffling, perplexing, incomprehensible, unexplainable, and unfathomable.* The story about the magic butterfly would fit this definition well and was mysterious enough. However, the very next day, I had something even more bizarre happen that fits this next definition of mysterious: *curious, puzzling, amazing, exciting, and awe inspiring.* In fact, God took me from curious, to puzzled, to amazed, to excited, and finally in awe of His mysterious power. Let me explain.

Curious

July 17

I woke up, had a cup of coffee, and headed to the pool. I wish I could say that I was on the lookout for God to do something mysterious, but after the puzzling event with the magic-butterfly the day before, I wasn't expecting anything new and outrageous. However, as I walked to the hot tub, I saw a wild spinning motion in the pool. It's hard to explain, but the motion appeared fantastically illuminated. The way the light reflected off the water, it almost looked like a cartoon picture of a miniature tornado submerged in the pool. I quickly jumped into the water and swam toward the strange activity. As I approached the spastic motion, I could see it was a big moth spinning out of control.

As I got closer to the moth, I could see he was spinning wildly in the water. But right before I reached him, I saw a very small piece of bark in front of the moth. For some funny reason, I decided to lift the little piece of wood out of the water before I lifted the big moth to safety. Oddly enough, as I picked up the bark and threw it about a foot away from me to the edge of the pool, it appeared to have magically split off into the form of a grasshopper! I didn't see a grasshopper on top of this tiny piece of bark or by the side of the pool when I picked it up and threw the bark. In fact, I don't even think the grasshopper could've fit on top of the itty-bitty piece of bark. However, when I threw it to the side of the pool, there was a little piece of bark and this mysterious grasshopper right next to it on the concrete.

My first thought was that the grasshopper must have been on top of the small piece of bark but fully blended in, and I just didn't recognize it. I took my attention back to the big moth that was still spinning out of control in circles and at a very rapid pace. I gently picked up the big moth and placed him about a foot away from the mysterious grasshopper on the side of the pool when I suddenly noticed a stranded bee near both of them.

Puzzled

As I swam away, I was a little puzzled because the spinning in the water didn't look natural to me when I first glanced at it. It was illuminated and stood out in a way that it appeared almost separated from the water. In other words, it seemed set apart from the rest of the pool in both color and movement. Unsure of what had just happened, I swam to the end of the pool. On my way back from the first lap, I decided to take a closer look at the spinning moth, the stranded bee, and the lifeless grasshopper. I noticed the grasshopper sat there completely motionless. In fact, I thought he was dead because he should've been hopping around or at the very least had some kind of movement. I swam to the other end of the pool and once again, I immediately came back to see the motionless grasshopper. He was alive but appeared lifeless. The bee was still stranded, and the moth was proudly prancing around. Trust me; it was a remarkably interesting sight!

Amazed

Immediately after I left the spot where the three insects were, I decided to go to the hot tub that's next to the pool. As I sat in my favorite place in the hot tub, I turned around. Lo and behold, there was a lifeless grasshopper next to a small piece of bark. This scene by the hot tub looked exactly like the one at the side of the pool! At first, I was thinking it was just another random grasshopper next to a random piece of bark. But then, a few seconds later, it occurred to me that I should go see the other grasshopper and bark by the poolside, just to make sure they were still there. I jumped out of the hot tub and swam quickly to the previous spot.

Lo and behold, the grasshopper and the piece of bark were both gone from the spot I had just left them! In a state of amazement, I thought, *I've got to look around and see if that lifeless grasshopper was hopping around somewhere.* I also looked to see if the wind had blown the little piece of bark, but no wind was blowing. I looked everywhere, and there was no grasshopper or bark to be found in the vicinity of the poolside or in the pool; both had literally disappeared!

Excited

I decided to take pictures like I did of the magic butterfly the day before. Sadly, I had forgotten to bring my cell phone to the pool. I hurried back to the apartment, grabbed my phone, and went to the hot tub. When I arrived, the lifeless grasshopper was still sitting there motionless right next to the little piece of bark. Like a good detective, I took pictures of everything. Lo and behold, it was only about a couple minutes after I was in the pool looking carefully at the prancing moth, the motionless grasshopper, and the lifeless bark when they all but vanished. And yes, the stranded bee was gone too!

In Awe of God's Power

It's curious as I would never have imagined God using insects to perform these supernatural events, but His ways are a mystery—difficult to understand, impossible to explain. I'm smiling as I type all of this because these were no mere bugs. It's funny to say, but I believe that God gave each of these little critters their own special powers to be displayed right in front of my eyes.

Let's review. It was only the day before that I saved the tiny butterfly two separate times in the pool. On the second save, it was *perplexing* and quite amazing that the little butterfly stayed in the palm of my hand in the pool, and then back into the hot tub. It was even more amazing to me that the little magic butterfly also stayed with me fifteen minutes later on my walk back to the apartment. The *unexplainable* part was that I absolutely knew that the magic butterfly was going to stay in the palm of my hand all the way back to my apartment.

Lo and behold, (abracadabra), the miniature butterfly disappeared from my left hand that was raised far above my head and somehow emerged out of the very bottom of the laundry I had just dumped on the couch with my right hand. Then, the miniature magic butterfly hung around outside on the back deck for over an hour until I showed Joni, which was right before he finally flew away. I kept saying out loud, "Are you kidding me!" but with a big smile on my face.

Then, the day after the magic butterfly incident, I unexpectedly saw a *peculiar* site; a wild spinning movement in the pool. It was illuminated inside the pool in such a way as to be an *unexplainable* yet a spectacular sight. It looked like a mini tornado and as *unfathomable* as this may sound, it was spinning in such a way as if it was actually trying to get my attention. As I approached it, I saw a big moth trapped in the water. I went over to rescue the spinning moth, but I threw a tiny piece of bark out of the pool first. Inexplicably, this little piece of bark seemed to split in two with one-part bark and the other part a lifeless grasshopper! This is exactly how it all happened.

The prancing moth and the motionless grasshopper both were on the side of the pool and stared directly at me when I stopped to check in on them. But here's the amazing part. Only seconds later, I went about twenty-five yards from the center of the pool to the hot tub after just having looked at the motionless grasshopper next to the tiny bark. Interestingly, I see the exact same grasshopper and bark right in front of my eyes at the hot tub! Within thirty seconds, I went to the pool to see if the grasshopper and the bark were back at the spot I had just left. Lo and behold, the motionless grasshopper was gone but amazingly enough so was the piece of bark! I looked all around the edge of the pool and inside the pool for both and found nothing. No bark, no grasshopper, and no moth.

I had two mysterious events in back-to-back days with bugs that appeared to possess mystical powers! For the record, no people were at the pool, so no one could have picked up the grasshopper or the bark. There was no wind at the pool site, so the bark was not blown away, but I still looked all around the area just in case. There you have it, on back-to-back days, God took me from curious, to puzzled, to amazed, to excited and finally in awe of His mysterious ways. It's a wonderful thing to experience the mysterious, and the last two days have been fantastic gifts of the mysterious to me.

God answered my original prayer several months ago, which was to allow me to prove his power to perform miracles in the present moment. As I finished typing these stories, I was filled with tears as the power of the Holy Spirit filled me with perfect peace, immense love, and overwhelming joy. I literally felt His presence in my midst as I typed these God stories for you. What a wonderful gift from God!

The Motionless Grasshopper Returns

August 22

I went swimming at the second pool at the apartment complex. Once again, I had the pool to myself. I was doing laps in the pool and thinking about God with all his magical bugs when lo and behold, the motionless grasshopper returned! I was praying and swimming with my eyes closed and when I opened my eyes, I was startled. I saw a motionless grasshopper on the top of a volleyball floating in the pool and directly in front of my face!

Funny enough, the grasshopper was lifeless, as he never moved. I even picked up the volleyball and placed it to the side of the pool. I leaned the ball all the way over to the point where he was touching the ground, but he would not budge! Between laps in the pool, I kept returning to check up on him. Eventually he was nowhere to be found.

In summary, God works in mysterious ways. He used the tiny magic butterfly, the motionless grasshopper, the flying piece of bark, and the prancing moth to take me from curious, to puzzled, to amazed, to excited, and finally in awe of His mystical powers.

CHAPTER TEN

God Is Wooing Us

> For ever since the creation of the world His invisible nature and attributes, that is, His eternal power and divinity, have been made intelligible and clearly discernible in and through the things that have been made [His handiworks]. So, [men] are without excuse [altogether without any defense or justification].
>
> **—Romans 1:20 AMP**

The spiritual journey God had me on included its own set of divine revelations along with new surprising supernatural events. Let me give you some more evidence to show that God is wooing us. I will attempt to do this first with my journal notes of some God stories from my random Bible openings in February. Then, I will share two more mysterious miracles that happened as I was near the home stretch of typing this book.

February 1

I read in my *Life of Christ* book this morning where the Pharisees asked Jesus to prove His divinity. Here's the story straight out of the Joyce Meyer *Everyday Life Bible*:

Then some of the scribes and Pharisees said to Him, Teacher, we desire to see a sign *or* miracle from You. [Proving that You are what You claim to be].

But He replied to them, An evil and adulterous generation [a generation morally unfaithful to God] seeks and demands a sign; but no sign shall be given to it except the sign of the prophet Jonah.

For even as Jonah was three days and three nights in the belly of the sea monster, so will the Son of Man be three days and three nights in the heart of the earth.

The men of Nineveh will stand up at the judgement with this generation and condemn it; for they repented at the preaching of Jonah, and behold, Someone more and greater than Jonah is here! (Mathew 12:38–41 AMP)

The last sentence had me visualizing Jesus saying, "Behold, Someone more and greater than Jonah is here!" Then I said a prayer and was bold enough to ask the Lord for a sign.

Lo and behold, I closed my eyes and did my random Bible opening where Jesus took me exactly to Jonah 3:3! Once again, I was filled with the Holy Spirit immediately after turning to Jonah. I wept in joy knowing that Jesus was with me. Here it is:

So Jonah arose and went to Nineveh according to the word of the Lord. Now Nineveh was an exceedingly great city of three days' journey [sixty miles in circumference]. (Jonah 3:3 AMP)

February 6

I was pondering my challenging set of circumstances over the last several years. I did my random Bible opening and asked God what he wanted to tell me this morning. Lo and behold, with my eyes closed, flipping the Bible around in my hands, I once again opened directly to Jonah. My eyes went to Joyce Meyer *Putting the Word to Work*, where Joyce wrote:

> Are you in unusual or difficult circumstances? Jonah certainly felt that way in the belly of the whale, yet God was using those circumstances to get his attention. No matter how desperate or hopeless your situation, no matter how far away God seems, know that God hears your prayers and will help you.

Perfect! Joyce's words were spot-on as to what I was feeling about the unusual set of difficult circumstances I've been in for quite some time (divorce, poverty, and no relationship with my two daughters). In my miracle journal I wrote, "God is most certainly getting my full attention!"

February 7

This morning I decided to read from another one of my favorite Christian books, *The Way to Love*, by the late Anthony De Mello. He spoke specifically about not being an insecure person. This same morning, I read in my *Life of Christ* book about the last parable of Christ on "the chaff."

Lo and behold, on my very last reading in my Hour of Spiritual Power, I just happened to read where I last left off from the book *The Wisdom of God*.

> The wicked are not so but are like chaff that the wind drives away. (Psalm 1:4)

The author, Nancy Guthrie, goes on to say:

> The chaff is worthless, lightweight, and disposable and simply blew away in the wind. There are two kinds of people the Psalmist sets before us: two kinds of people living in two different ways. One is secure, invulnerable to whatever winds might blow. The other is insecure and unsubstantial, vulnerable to being carried away by the wind into nothingness.

This had me thinking about the future and how unbelievers will be blown away into nothingness. I got down on my knees and prayed, God, please reveal to me something about the future. Lo and behold, with my eyes closed and flipping the Bible all around in my hands, I opened randomly to Ezekiel 30.

> For the day is near, even the day of the Lord, a cloudy day; it shall be the time [of doom] for the nations. (Ezekiel 30:1–3 AMP)

Now this random Bible opening really got my attention. In fact, it shook me up enough that I had to go for a long walk to think about it. You see, I became a published author back in 2008. However, I wrote my first self-published book in 2007, also titled *Discover the Upside of Down*, where I was predicting a stock and real estate crash, which indeed happened in 2008 and 2009. At the time of this random Bible opening, I was working on my next stock market book titled *Rediscover the Upside of Down*, with the subtitle *Here We Go Again!*

In my new financial book, I am making similar predictions as in the Wiley published book but with one big exception. I predict an economic catastrophe with multiple nations around the world defaulting on their enormous debt loads, which I believe will result in the new Great Depression of the twenty-first century. When I read the random Bible opening to Ezekiel: "the day of doom for all nations is near," it hit me hard because I see economic doom for all nations with unhealthy levels of debt. Somewhere in the future, five to fifteen years perhaps, giant debtor nations like the U.S.A., Japan, and much of Europe, will collapse economically. I see this kind of doom as a high probability event.

The question for me is not if but when. My newest stock market manuscript, which I plan to publish, predicts all nations that printed, borrowed, and spent excessively will be doomed to default. There's simply no other answer except mass debt defaults resulting from the excess buildup of nearly $300 trillion worth of global government debt.

February 8

I normally sleep eight hours per night most of the time. It's one of the many wonderful blessings God bestowed upon me. However, on this night, I woke up at two o'clock with bad thoughts about my divorce. I saw my Bible on the table and said out loud; "God, what do you have to say about this bad dream?" Lo and behold, (believe it or not) my random Bible opening had me go to Proverbs where my eyes landed on Proverbs 12:4. My jaw hit the floor as this Bible opening sent me into a near state of shock!

> A virtuous and worthy wife [earnest and strong in character] is a crowning joy to her husband, but she who makes him ashamed is as rottenness in his bones. (Proverbs 12:4 AMP)

February 10

As part of my daily Hour of Spiritual Power, I would read Joel Osteen's *2015 Devotional Calendar*. Today, Joel used a quote I absolutely loved:

> "For I know the plans I have for you," says the Lord. "They are plans for good and not for disaster, to give you a future and a hope." (Jeremiah 29:11 NLT)

In "Today's Word" of his devotional calendar, Joel talks about "pruning the dream crashers" from your life to "make room to surround yourself with the right people." I liked reading this because it was a decision that I had made years earlier to prune all unhealthy relationships. After reading this and praying, I did my random Bible opening. Lo and behold, I went directly to Jeremiah 17:9 (AMP):

> The heart is deceitful above all things, and it is exceedingly perverse [and] corrupt and severely, mortally sick! Who can know it [perceive, understand, be acquainted with his own heart and mind]?

February 11
As part of my daily hour with the Lord, I had just finished reading in my yellow miracle notebook about how I defined wisdom as putting God behind all my goals (Power Goals). Right after reading on wisdom, I prayed: *Lord, please keep teaching me more of Your Wisdom. Amen.* Lo and behold, with my eyes closed, I did the random Bible opening where my eyes opened to Job 28:28: "But to man He said, Behold, the reverential and worshipful fear of the Lord that is Wisdom; and to depart from evil is understanding." And my eyes then went to Job 28:23 (AMP): "God understands the way [to wisdom] and He knows the place of it [Wisdom is with God alone]." Here are a couple more Bible quotes from Job on wisdom:

> Gold and glass cannot equal [Wisdom], nor can it be exchanged for jewels or vessels of fine gold. (Job 28:17)

> No mention shall be made of coral or of crystal; for the possession of Wisdom is even above rubies and pearls. (Job 28:18)

Here's what Joyce Meyer said in *Putting the Word to Work*:

> Where do you seek wisdom? Do you understand
> its value? Job knew that the value of wisdom is far
> beyond wealth, and that wisdom is found in fearing
> the Lord (see Job 28:12–28). Ask the lord to teach
> you what it means to fear Him and to help you grow
> in wisdom.

February 14

I just finished reading in *The Life of Christ* book about how Jesus prayed
to God on blessing His disciples and protecting them from sin. Jesus
was preparing for His death only eighteen hours away. I felt extremely
moved as I read this. I imagined what Jesus must have been thinking as
He knew exactly what was ahead for Him on the cross, the persecution
ahead for His disciples, and His coming ascension to heaven. Feeling
the Holy Spirit upon me, I prayed; *Dear Jesus, please teach me something
on how You felt.* Lo and behold, I read exactly what Jesus felt after His
resurrection when "He reproved and reproached" the eleven disciples
for their lack of faith! This random Bible opening went to Mark 16
where my eyes went directly to: "The stone was already rolled back."
Here's the entire story that ends the Gospel of Mark:

> And when the Sabbath was past [that is, after the sun
> had set], Mary Magdalene, and Mary [the mother of
> James], and Salome purchased sweet-smelling spices,
> so that they might go and anoint [Jesus's body].
>
> And very early on the first day of the week they
> came to the tomb; [by then] the sun had risen.
>
> And they said to one another, Who will roll back
> the stone for us out of [the grooves across the floor
> at] the door of the tomb?

And when they looked up, they [distinctly] saw that the stone was already rolled back, for it was very large.

And going into the tomb, they saw a young man sitting [there] on the right [side], clothed in a [long, stately, sweeping] robe of white, and they were utterly amazed *and* struck with terror.

And he said to them, Do not be amazed *and* terrified; you are looking for Jesus of Nazareth, Who was crucified. He has risen; He is not here. See the place where they laid Him.

But be going; tell the disciples and Peter, He goes before you into Galilee; you will see Him there [just] as He told you.

Then they went out [and] fled from the tomb, for trembling and bewilderment *and* consternation had seized them. And they said nothing about it to anyone, for they were by alarm *and* fear.

Now Jesus, having risen [from death] early on the first day of the week, appeared first to Mary Magdalene, from whom He had driven out seven demons.

She went and reported it to those who had been with Him, as they grieved and wept.

And when they heard that He was alive and that she had seen Him, they did not believe it.

After this, He appeared in a different form to two of them as they were walking [along the way] into the country.

And they returned [to Jerusalem] and told the others, but they did not believe them either.

Afterward He appeared to the eleven [apostles themselves] as they reclined at table; and He reproved *and* reproached them for their unbelief [their lack of faith] and their hardness of heart, because they had refused to believe those who had seen Him *and* looked at Him attentively after He had risen [from death].

And He said to them, Go into all the world and preach *and* publish openly the good news [the Gospel] to every creature [of the whole human race].

He who believes [who adheres to and trusts in and relies on the Gospel and Him Whom it sets forth] and is baptized will be saved [from the penalty of eternal death]; but he who does not believe [who does not adhere to and trust in and rely on the Gospel and Him Whom it sets forth] will be condemned.

And these attesting signs will accompany those who believe in My name they will drive out demons; they will speak in new languages;

They will pick up serpents; and [even] if they drink anything deadly it will not hurt them; they will lay their hands on the sick, and they will get well.

So then the Lord Jesus, after He spoken to them, was taken up into heaven and He sat down at the right hand of God.

And they went out and preached everywhere, while the Lord kept working with them and confirming the message by the attesting signs *and* miracles that closely accompanied [it]. Amen [so be it]. (Mark 16:1–20 AMP)

Joyce Meyer Life Point in the *Everyday Life Bible* says:

Mark 16:20 says that the apostles went everywhere preaching the Word and God confirmed the Word with signs and miracles. I always believed those signs and wonders to be miraculous healings until God began showing me to believe not only for miraculous healings to confirm the Word preached, but also to believe for and expect miraculous breakthroughs and abundant fruit in whatever area I was ministering. Whatever you do to serve the Lord, believe God for miraculous breakthroughs to follow the things you do to serve Him. When we are about His business, we can expect signs and wonders to follow us."

Joyce is correct, as this book has shown that miraculous breakthroughs along with signs and wonders are a natural experience when you walk in faith with God.

July 28

Today's Word in Joel Osteen's *Devotional Calendar* is very coincidental to the story that happened to me on this very same day: "Faith is the confidence that what we hope for will actually happen; it gives us assurance about things we cannot see" (Hebrews 11:1 NLT).

I went to the pool and during my daily swim, I was attracted to a dead bee. For some strange reason I decided to ask God to bring the dead bee back to life. I know this sounds absurd, but God had been working miracles around mysterious insects: the magic butterfly, the spinning moth, and the mystical grasshopper. Why not ask God to bring the dead bee back to life? At the time, it seemed logical for me to ask God.

Anyway, I was swimming next to the bee by the edge of the pool asking God to bring him back to life. I swam to the other end of the pool and back, only to see the lifeless bee still melted and stuck on the hot cement. Once again, I prayed; *Please God, you've been doing all these miracles with bugs, and this one would be a great story for the book You asked me to write.* I did another lap but still the dead bee was as dead as ever.

I went over to the hot tub and looked at that bee very carefully. I couldn't help but stare at it. I said another little prayer; *Please, God?* Then the heat from the hot tub and the sun was too much for me. As I stood up to go back to my apartment, I looked at the dead-bee at my feet when I said one more prayer; *Lord, I'm leaving now; can you please do something with that dead bee?* Then, I put my towel up to my face and wiped some water from my eyes, and two seconds later I looked over to the dead bee.

Lo and behold, *poof*! The dead bee was gone! I shouted in amazement, "Are you kidding me!" I looked everywhere, and there was no bee to be found. He was not blown away in the pool, as there was no wind and besides, he appeared to be melted tightly to the concrete, which was several feet from the pool. He wasn't anywhere around the wide-open concrete area. He was simply gone! I was left standing in a state of bewilderment. I left the pool shaking my head wondering how many more miracle bug stories were left for this book. Lo and behold …

July 30

On this day, I didn't get to the main pool like I normally do. When that happens, I go over to the other pool because it's rarely used. As I jumped into the pool that afternoon, I had a strong feeling God was going to do another miracle.

I noticed a blue volleyball in the pool. I decided to throw it about fifteen feet from me, and it drifted right back. I did this again, and once again, it drifted back to me. I wondered if God was going to do something with the volleyball. But then I thought the ball was a distraction because it wasn't a bug. I picked up the volleyball and threw it about twenty-five feet near the center of the pool.

In great anticipation, I went back to swimming laps. I kept looking all around the pool to see what was surrounding me. There was absolutely nothing in the pool and nothing I could see around it except some doves flying far above me. As I was returning to complete the lap, I had this strong feeling God was up to something. Suddenly, on this calm and quiet day, the winds started to kick up, and the pool water got extremely choppy. Also, the sun temporarily fell behind a dark cloud as I started to swim back to the last spot where I had thrown the blue volleyball.

Lo and behold, I was absolutely startled to see a long skinny lizard two inches from my face! In a state of bewilderment, I immediately started laughing out loud as I jumped out of the pool to get my cell phone to take pictures of the little lizard. Then, I put my phone away to rescue him from the water. I pushed him to the side, but he kept bumping his head into the rim at the edge of the pool. I grabbed his long tail, but he startled me, and I dropped him in the pool. Then, I coupled my hands together with water underneath him and carefully tossed him to the concrete on the side of the pool. Lo and behold, in midair, he disappeared right in front of my eyes! *Poof!* He was gone. I looked everywhere around the pool just to make sure my mind wasn't playing tricks on me. I found no sign of the disappearing lizard. Abracadabra: the skinny lizard was gone and nowhere to be found.

What Does It All Mean?

Right before I started to write this book, I asked God for clear instructions of how to proceed, and I clearly heard: **Write it All in a book.** I share all these supernatural experiences with you as

I was instructed to do, but what's the meaning behind it all? One explanation I have is that God was giving me some cool miracle stories to build a solid proof statement of His mystical powers for this book. When you really think about it, it makes sense that God would perform wonders and miracles as I typed this book in honor of Him, His Son Jesus Christ, and the Holy Spirit.

Joni had her theory on the magic butterfly that stayed calmly in the palm of my hand. She felt that I was the tiny butterfly in the palm of God's hand. As far as the little guy emerging from my dirty laundry I had dumped on the couch, she had this to say: "Ron, the Bible speaks all about us being in the palm of God's hand. I believe you are the little butterfly in this miracle story, and God showed you that you are in the palm of His hand. I also believe God showed you that as the butterfly emerged from beneath the clothes, you too will emerge from the mountain of problems that have covered you the last several years."

As I thought about it some more, that insightful statement made perfect sense to me. It also occurred to me that as confidently and calmly as the little butterfly was in my hand is just how I've always felt with my life being in God's hand. I've always felt confident that God is directing my path. As I type this book, I've never been more confident of that fact.

The spinning moth, the magic butterfly, and the disappearing lizard all had one thing in common; I went into the water to save each of them from drowning. Even the dead bee on the side of the pool I wanted God to bring back to life, and I believe that He did! My buddy Paul told me that I liked to "save people" when they were in a deep emotional crisis. That may be true, but apparently it extends to insects, rodents, and even dead bees!

However, in this case, God clearly was reminding me that He saved me every single time I wound up in hot water. He also reminded me of the great miracles that He had performed in the past by doing more in the present moment at the time I was writing this book. Finally, maybe God demonstrated these mysterious wonders for those who read this book to pay close attention to the words of wisdom He revealed to me. I'm also considering turning these mysterious bug stories into a children's book.

In summary, I decided to go directly to the source of these miracles. In a prayer, I asked God why He used insects and a lizard to perform signs and wonders before my eyes. I specifically asked Him to reveal to me in a random Bible opening what it all meant. Lo and behold, I closed my eyes and opened to the quote I featured at the beginning of this chapter! Believe it or not, God had my eyes go directly to Romans 1:20 for the specific answer to my prayer. In Romans 1:20, God speaks about His "invisible nature and attributes" and about His "eternal power having been made intelligible and clearly discernible in and through the things that He made." Joyce Meyer describes "the thing's He made" as "God's handiworks." Certainly, bugs and lizards are things God made. Once again, God answered perfectly in my random Bible opening as He showed me "His eternal power through the things He made."

CHAPTER ELEVEN

God Is Available

The Bible story in 1 Kings best describes the way God speaks to those who believe in Him. Elijah the prophet had just slain 450 false prophets of their false god named Baal. This was after Elijah had proved to the people that Baal was a false god while he also proved the power, existence, and reality of the God of Abraham, Isaac, and Israel (1 Kings 18:18–40). After the slaughtering, Elijah was exhausted, stressed, and hiding in a cave. Here's the story in 1 Kings 19:9–12 (AMP):

> There he came to a cave and lodged in it; and behold, the word of the Lord came to him, and He said to him, What are you doing here, Elijah?
>
> He replied, I have been very jealous for the Lord God of hosts; for the Israelites have forsaken Your covenant, thrown down Your altars, and killed Your prophets with the sword. And I, I only, am left; and they seek my life, to take it away.
>
> And He said, Go out and stand on the mount before the Lord. And behold, the Lord passed by, and a great and strong wind rent the mountains and broke

in pieces the rocks before the Lord, but the Lord was not in the wind; and after the wind an earthquake, but the Lord was not in the earthquake;

And after the earthquake a fire, but the Lord was not in the fire, and after the fire [a sound of gentle stillness and] a still, small voice.

The Spiritual Journey Continues

February 15
I was reading in my yellow miracle notebook about eternity. I noted the importance of "living for God by serving, believing, and loving His Son Jesus Christ." In prayer, I felt a strong urge to ask the Lord to reveal more to me on eternity.

Lo and behold, I closed my eyes and did my random Bible opening where I went directly to Psalm 119:92 where it speaks about living for God and his Word, and as you read on, the word *eternity* is mentioned in my Joyce Meyer *Everyday Life Bible*.

Unless your law had been my delight, I would have perished in my affliction.

I will never forget your precepts for it is by them you have quickened me.

I am yours therefore save me; for I have sought Your precepts and required them.

The wicked wait for me to destroy me, but I will consider Your testimonies.

I have seen that everything has its limits and end, but your commandment is exceedingly broad and extends without limits (into eternity). (Psalm 119:92–96 AMP)

February 17

I simply asked God to reveal what he wanted to teach me today. Apparently, we weren't done with the previous day on eternity. Lo and behold, I did my random Bible opening where my eyes went to Romans 2:6–8 (AMP):

> For He will render to every man according to his works [justly, as his deeds deserve]. To those who by patient persistence in well-doing [springing from piety] seek [unseen but sure] glory and honor and [the eternal blessedness of] immortality, He will give eternal life. But for those who are self-seeking and self-willed and disobedient to the Truth but responsive to wickedness, there will be indignation and wrath.

February 18

I just finished reading *The Life of Christ* where the author distinguishes between Judas, who betrayed Jesus, and Peter, who denied Jesus three times: "Peter was filled with repentance while Judas was filled with remorse. Repentance is not concerned with consequences; but remorse is inspired principally by fear of consequences."

On this same day, I also read about King David repenting for sleeping with Bathsheba and then having her husband killed in battle. In my morning prayer, I asked God to reveal to me in a random Bible opening about all I had read on repentance. Lo and behold, I opened to Revelation 2:5 where there is much to be said about repenting for sins!

> Remember then from what heights you have fallen. Repent (change the inner man to meet God's will) and do the works you did previously [when first you knew the Lord], or else I will visit you and remove your lampstand from its place, unless you change your mind and repent. (Revelation 2:5 AMP)

February 21

I had just finished reading in *The Life of Christ* about Jesus being crucified and how He fulfilled all prophecies that Isaiah had foretold about Him. The prophecy in *The Life of Christ* book specifically referred to Isaiah on the coming destruction of Israel. Lo and behold, I randomly opened to Luke 23:27–30 in my Everyday Life Bible.

> And there accompanied [Jesus] a great multitude of the people, [including] women who bewailed and lamented Him. But Jesus, turning toward them, said, Daughters of Jerusalem, do not weep for Me, but weep for yourselves and for your children. For behold, the days are coming during which they will say, Blessed (happy, fortunate, and to be envied) are the barren, and the wombs that have not borne, and the breasts that have never nursed [babies]! Then they will begin to say to the mountains, Fall on us! and to the hills, Cover (conceal, hide) us!

After reading this I was moved. I said a quiet prayer and quickly opened the Bible with absolutely no thought other than Jesus would show me again something related to what I just read and how I was feeling in the present moment. Lo and behold, my random Bible opening took me precisely to Isaiah 5. This is the chapter where the prophet shows Israel their transgressions and the judgments to be brought upon them for their sins and the ruin that God warned as a justified punishment. This verse in Isaiah sums up the chapter well in relation to what Jesus told the weeping women on the day Jesus was crucified.

> Therefore is the anger of the Lord kindled against His people, and He has stretched forth His hand against them and has smitten them. And the mountains trembled, and their dead bodies were like dung *and*

sweepings in the midst of the streets. For all this, His anger is not turned away, but His hand is still stretched out (in judgment). (Isaiah 5:25 AMP)

God Answers Prayers

For where two or three are gathered together in my name, there am I in the midst of them. (Matthew 18:20 KJV)

February 25

Joni was in a job that brought her quite a bit of unhappiness and anxiety. As so often is the case in a bad job, a person treated her poorly and troubled her greatly. Joni desperately wanted out. We decided to pray about getting a new job. Also, for a multitude of reasons, we both decided that it was time to leave Southern Oregon, and we both desired to live in Arizona. This was the first time that Joni and I were physically together in prayer. As I mentioned earlier, while I lived in Bend, and Joni lived in Medford, we would often pray at 7:30 a.m. on specific topics and situations.

On this day, we sat on her couch and held hands as she led the prayer: "Lord, I'm asking that You please take me out of this job and help me get a better job in Arizona. Today, I claim Your promises, and I thank You for making this happen." I repeated some of what Joni asked but I also prayed; "Lord, You said that when two or more are gathered in Your name that You would be with them. Thank You for being here in our midst right now, and thank You for hearing our prayers. Amen."

Lo and behold, only a few weeks later, Joni was let go from her job as her position was eliminated in a cost-cutting decision by the employer. Coincidently, on the same day Joni was let go, she had her first interview with a company in Chandler, Arizona. About one month after her first interview, Joni was working in her new job in Arizona.

I can tell you without a shadow of a doubt that we both felt the Lord's presence in that few minutes of our deep and sincere prayer. We believed that our prayers would be answered as we already had several prayers answered. You can trust and believe in this promise from Jesus: For where two or three are gathered together in My name, there am I in the midst of them.

Here's another recent miracle story that relates to the promise of what happens when two or three are gathered in the name of Jesus. I was sharing a couple of my God stories with a gentleman named Robert. He is a Christian, but he was still amazed at my miracle stories. Then, he told me about his grave concern with his left leg. He said that he was in a lot of pain. He asked me if I would pray for his healing. I agreed and then I held him close and prayed to Jesus for his leg to be healed, and I quoted some of Matthew 18:19 in my prayer: *Lord Jesus, You promised that where two or three are gathered together in Your name, that You are with us as we pray. I ask that You please relieve Robert's pain and ultimately heal his leg. Amen.*

One week later, I received this text from Robert when I asked him about his leg: "Ron, I was told that I might have a blood clot in my right leg, which of course concerned me. Then sometime after that, you and I prayed together. I had a sonogram on Tuesday and there is no blood clot! They were able to diagnose what was causing the problem. My thinking is I may have very well had a blood clot, and I got healed. Thank you for praying for me."

February 26

I had just finished reading in my miracle binder about a "Spiritual Army." I felt an urge to pray, but before I did, I performed a ritual. I brushed my teeth, showered, put baby powder all over my body, fresh new deodorant, new clean socks, and I even flossed. Then, I got on my hands and knees, put my face to the ground, and prayed out loud: "Dear Jesus, thank You for making my soul clean by dying on Your cross and forgiving me of my sins." After all of this, I picked up my Bible, closed my eyes, and did my random Bible opening. Lo and behold, I opened directly to Ephesians 6 where I saw: Spiritual Army, Spiritual War, Spiritual Forces, Spiritual Enemy, and Spiritual Armor all over the page!

> Put on God's whole armor [the armor of a heavy-armed soldier, which God supplies], that you may be able successfully to stand up against [all] the strategies *and* the deceits of the devil. (Ephesians 6:11 AMP)

> Therefore put on God's complete armor, that you may be able to resist *and* stand your ground on the evil day [of danger], and, having done all [the crisis demands], to stand [firmly in your place]. (Ephesians 6:13)

> And take the helmet of salvation and the sword that the Spirit wields, which is the Word of God. (Ephesians 6:17)

February 27

I had just finished reading my notes where I wrote, "God has done excellent surgery on my heart, but it's been painful." In other words, God tested me and my faith in very challenging ways over the previous many years. I then prayed and picked up my Bible, closed my eyes, and did my random Bible opening. Lo and behold, I opened directly to Zachariah where Joyce Meyer wrote: "Have you ever heard the saying, trial by fire?" She then suggested turning to Zachariah 13:9: "And I will bring the third part through the fire and will refine them as silver and will test them as gold is tested."

February 28

I started my daily hour with Jesus and my stomach started growling. Normally I would have responded to my hunger, but instead I made a conscious choice to seek the Word of God. I made this decision as I was thinking about how Jesus resisted Satan who tempted our Lord when He was hungry. I picked up my journal and once again read about "putting on the Armor of God when the enemy attacks our spirit." Then, out of the blue, I had a strong impression to read one page beyond where I left off the previous day in Ezra. Lo and behold, I read Ezra 8:3 where Joyce Meyer in *Putting the Word to Work* wrote: "Are you facing a challenging situation and opposition from the enemy?" Joyce on the next page in her commentary titled; "Seek God Desperately":

> In Ezra 8:23, we read Ezra proclaimed a fast to show his desperation to God when the Israelites required protection and needed to know what to do. Missing a few meals and taking that time to seek God is not a bad idea. Ezra and the Israelites "besought" God (Ezra 8:23), which simply means they sought Him, and they inquired of Him. When we seek God, we pursue, crave, and go search for food to keep us alive. We need to seek God all the time, not just when we are in trouble.

In summary, God continued to enrich my soul in February. As you read on, you will eventually see how this all leads up to a series of life-altering events for me. There is no greater wisdom than from the Old Testament and the New Testament. There was absolutely no doubt in my mind that each month on this spiritual journey, God was answering my direct prayer for wisdom. To my spiritual delight and satisfaction, God answered when I asked Him to prove His power to perform miracles for this book. God is with us; He answers prayers; He performs miracles, even instant miracles. He certainly proved all of that and much more to me, especially as time wore on. In other words, this was just the tip of the iceberg as far as what additional miracles God was about to show me.

CHAPTER TWELVE

God Is Wisdom

Save me, O God, by thy name, and judge me by thy strength. Hear my prayer, O God; give ear to the words of my mouth.

—Psalm 54 KJV

Every morning in the new year, I started my *Hour of Spiritual Power* off by reading *Today's Word Devotional Calendar* by Joel and Victoria Osteen. However, it was the month of March when Joel played a bigger role in my random Bible openings.

March 1

Today's word in the devotional calendar was from Psalm 31:15: "My times are in your hands." Joel comments:

> Throughout the Psalms, David acknowledges that he chose to put his life in the hands of the Lord. In this verse, he was saying, I trust You God, because I know You are good, my times are in Your hands. Are you willing to release every area of your life to the Father? Are you willing to trust Him with

the times and seasons of your life? You may be in a situation that you don't fully understand, but take heart, God is a good God, and you can trust Him. He is working behind the scenes on your behalf.

Joel and Victoria have a place in the daily calendar to journal thoughts. Here is what I wrote on March 1:

It has been a rocky road for me, but Jesus brought me to exactly where he wanted my heart. I had been asking the Lord for peace and joy but in order for that to happen, He had to strip away all my unhealthy attachments. But through it all, I never lost my faith. At times, I certainly lost my way, but I never lost my faith or my love for Jesus Christ. I trust Him even though so much has been lost, but it's clear to see that it was all for my spiritual gain.

After writing this down, I did a random Bible opening. Lo and behold, I open to the most perfect spot in the Joyce Meyer *Everyday Life Bible*—the front of Job. Here is Joyce Meyer's introduction to the story of Job.

Simply put, the book of Job is about hard times. It teaches us that God does allow His people to suffer at times, but it also reminds us that God is with us in the midst of our suffering and encourages us to cling to Him through it all, no matter what we face in life.

Job endured almost every kind of loss imaginable—money, possessions, family, health, and the support of his friends. He did not lose his hope in God even when things became so bad that his wife wanted him to "renounce God and die!" but Job called her foolish and responded: "Shall we accept (only) good at the hand of God and shall we not accept (also) misfortune …?" (Job 2:9–10 AMP).

Verse 10 in Job continues: "In (spite of) all this, Job did not sin with his lips. He remained faithful to God despite devastating and difficult circumstances. In the end, God rewarded Job's faithfulness and restored double what he had lost."

Joyce Meyer comments:

> Remember the lessons of Job when you face suffering in your life. Remember that God loves you, that your Redeemer lives and is working on your behalf, that nothing can steal God's presence from you, that you may have to close your ears to the skeptics in your life, that your preserving faith will ultimately cause you to triumph, and that God is able to restore far more than you have lost or suffered.

March 2

Every day for fifty straight days in my morning hour with the Lord, I would also read Joel's *50 Days to Better Living: A Day-to-Day Journal to Build Your Relationship to God*. Today's word from Joel: "Trust that your destiny supersedes your mistakes." Today's word from the Bible was Psalm 138:8 (NLT): "The Lord will work out His plans for my life-for your faithful love, O Lord, endures forever."

Here is what I typed in my journal: "I'm expecting my time of loss will soon be behind me and my time for gains is ahead of me. I will wait, listen and watch by thinking and praying with hopeful expectations." Lo and behold, I did a random Bible opening where my eyes went right to Hosea 12:6, which once again relates perfectly to what I wrote in my journal.

> Therefore, return to your God! Hold fast to love *and* mercy, to righteousness *and* justice, and wait

[expectantly] for your God continually! (Hosea 12:6 AMP)

March 3

I wrote new goals for March in my miracle notebook. For Spiritual Awareness, here's what I wrote: "I will live a spirit-filled life and become a new man in Christ." I then said a quick prayer and opened my Bible. Lo and behold (believe it or not), I went to Samuel on being turned into a new man, and I saw the word *Spirit* ten times on one page! Here's the Joyce Meyer commentary titled "Changed by the Spirit":

> When the Spirit of God truly comes upon a person, that person will be changed. First Samuel 10:6 tells us that Saul would be "turned into another man," which really means that he would be so thoroughly changed that people would think he was someone else. The most important evidence of a Spirit Filled life is a change of character and the development of the fruit of the Holy Spirit.

> Then the Spirit of the Lord will come upon you mightily, and you will show yourself to be a prophet with them; and you will be turned into another man. (1 Samuel 10:6 AMP)

March 4

I had just finished reading in my journals: "The move to Winthrop near the beautiful mountains saved my peace of mind." I then said a quick prayer and randomly opened my Bible. Lo and behold, I opened to Isaiah 55:12: "For you shall go out with joy and be led forth with peace; the mountains and the hills shall break forth before you with singing, and all the trees of the field shall clap their hands."

God Displays His Power

> And when they had prayed, the place in which they
> were assembled was shaken; and they were all filled
> with the Holy Spirit, and they continued to speak
> the Word of God with freedom and boldness and
> courage. (Acts 4:31 AMP)

It was a beautiful afternoon in Southern Oregon when I decided
to drive out to Cantrell Buckley, one of my favorite parks to go
think and pray. As is almost always the case, I brought my leather
workbag and my favorite folding chair with me. The reason I like
to go to this quiet park is because it's right on the Applegate River,
and there's rarely anyone there. On this day I had a lot on my mind.
To be more specific, I was still trying to figure out the best way to
move forward with my life.

I parked at my favorite spot by the river where I unloaded the
car. I found a shady spot about fifteen yards from the water. I opened
my folding chair and placed my workbag on a giant log. I was just
about to start reading my Bible when I decided to walk to the river
to wash my hands and face to feel cleansed. As I did this ceremonial
washing in the river, I prayed: *Thank you, Jesus, for washing me clean
of all my sins by dying on Your cross. I'm here to ask You what it is You
want me to do with my life. Amen.*

Lo and behold, at that very moment, I heard a loud crash behind
me! I was startled and immediately turned around only to see that
the wind had blown my heavy workbag off the giant log where I had
placed it! Immediately I thought, *Maybe that was God answering my
prayer somehow.*

My workbag is filled with my journals and lots of pens,
highlighters, and other stuff. In other words, my leather workbag is
always jam-packed full of books, files, and other stuff, which makes
it heavy and bulky. As I walked over to my workbag, I noticed about
twenty pens and highlighters had fallen out. I also saw that all my

index cards with my thoughts, plans, and goals had fallen out too. The very top index card that faced up at me after it fell out of the bag said, "Turn your life around by completing phase one," and it listed all the things that needed to be done to fully complete phase one.

The same index card said, "Go immediately to phase two after completing phase one," and then listed all the things to do in phase 2. Let me explain. Phase 1 stated something critically important that I had to get done in order to move forward with my life. Phase 2 happened to be a specific instruction I received from God in a vision. I wrote the instruction from God (my answer) under phase 2, and apparently God wanted His answer in front of my face versus stuffed inside my workbag. He reminded me of His original instruction, and He did it in dramatic fashion.

As is so often the case, I wanted God to confirm what just happened. I sat down with my Bible along with the index card in my hand, and I said a deeply sincere prayer: *God, please confirm in a random Bible opening that what just happened with my workbag was directly from you. Amen.* Lo and behold, with my eyes closed, I opened the Bible to Jonah 1:4: "But the Lord sent out a great wind upon the sea."

What I need to emphasize here is that the very second I finished my first prayer was when I heard the crash. I was shaken because my heavy workbag made a loud sound as it fell from the top of the giant log and hit the ground. Then, the exact answers to my prayer were placed right in front of my face on the index card. In other words, God answered instantly and powerfully! Finally, He confirmed it all perfectly in my random Bible opening during my second prayer! Here is what I wrote in my personal journal: "These events are real! I'm finally getting it. I feel humbled, a little scared, incredibly spirit-filled, excited, and, most importantly, I continue to feel confident God is with me, and He is guiding my life."

March 7

In Joel's *50 Days to Better Living* journal, Proverbs 17:22 (ASV): "A Cheerful Heart is good medicine." I then opened my journal notes and read the "God's Sense of Humor" story. I then said a prayer and opened my Bible randomly. Lo and behold, I go to Mathew 11:1–6, where I see the word *blessed* (happy) ten times on one page!

> And blessed (happy, fortunate, and to be envied) is he who takes no offense at Me and finds no cause for stumbling in or through Me and is not hindered from seeing the Truth. (Mathew 11:6 AMP)

And then … what happier of a passage for a believer than this:

> And Jesus replied to them, Go and report to John what you hear and see: The blind receive their sight and the lame walk, lepers are cleansed (by healing) and the deaf hear, the dead are raised up and the poor have good news (the Gospel) preached to them. (Matthew 11:4–5)

March 8

It was my birthday, and I was expecting something really good in my random Bible opening. As I mentioned, every day for fifty straight days, I started my hour with the Lord by also reading *Today's Word Devotional Calendar* by Joel Osteen, and here was the Bible quote Joel used on my birthday: "The thief comes only to steal and kill and destroy. I came that they may have life and have it abundantly" (John 10:10 ESV).

Today's Word from Joel: "Christ performed miracles in the Bible, and He is still doing miracles today. The Bible says He is the same yesterday, today and forever. No matter what weapon the enemy may throw at you, it cannot penetrate the defense that Christ has put around you! Guard your hope, your joy, and your victory in Christ because they are God-given blessings that He wants you to enjoy every day."

In Joel Osteen's *50 Days to Better Living;* the Bible quote also had the word *hope.*

Rejoice in our confident hope. Be patient in trouble and keep on praying. (Romans 12:12 AMP)

In the journal part I wrote, "always keep hope alive." Also, in my miracle journal, I was complaining about the fact that I knew neither of my two daughters would call me on my birthday. I felt bitterness as I was lamenting about how a difficult separation and divorce turned them away from me. At the end of it all, I prayed with hopeful expectations for a renewed relationship with my daughters someday. Lo and behold, I closed my eyes to do my random Bible opening and opened right to Lamentations 3!

> I am [Jeremiah] the man who has seen affliction under the rod of His wrath. (Lamentations 3:1 AMP)

> He has built up [siege mounds] against me and surrounded me with bitterness, tribulation, and anguish. (3:5)

> He has enclosed my ways with hewn stone; He has made my paths crooked. (3:9)

> He has filled me with bitterness; He has made me drink to excess and until drunken with wormwood [bitterness]. (3:15)

> He has also broken my teeth with gravel (stones). He has covered me with ashes. (3:16)

> But this I recall and therefore have I hope and expectation. (3:21)

> It is because of the Lord's mercy and loving-kindness that we are not consumed, because His [tender] compassions fail not. (3:22)

They are new every morning; great and abundant is Your stability and faithfulness. (3:23)

The Lord is my portion *or* share, says my living being (my inner self); therefore will I Hope in Him and wait expectantly for Him. (3:24)

The Lord is good to those who wait hopefully and expectantly for Him, to those who seek Him [inquire of and for Him and require Him by right of necessity and on the authority of God's word]. (3:25)

It is good that one should hope in and wait quietly for the salvation [the safety and ease] of the Lord. (3:26)

It is good for a man that he should bear the yoke [of divine disciplinary dealings] in his youth. (3:27)

Let him sit alone uncomplaining and keeping silent [in hope], because [God] has laid [the yoke] upon him [for his benefit]. (3:28)

Joyce Meyer writes in her *Life Point:* "The writer's positive thoughts about God brought him out of the depressed, miserable state he was in. When we think about our problems, we sink lower and lower, but thoughts about goodness, mercy, kindness and faithfulness of God gives us hope."

In summary, here's what I wrote in my journal: "God's birthday present to me was that I should indeed keep *hope* alive because someday He will reunite me with my daughters. I am simply to wait expectantly for the best from God by always trusting in Him and always trusting in His perfect timing."

March 9

I did my random Bible opening and opened to the back of the Joyce Meyer *Everyday Life Bible* where she has several blank pages for personal notes that she calls *Everyday Life Notes*. On day one of doing my first entries in this section, I wrote this from the Bible: 2 Peter 3:1: "I think it is right, as long as I am in this tabernacle, to stir you up by way of remembrance." It was time for me to remember all God had done for me. I found this way of remembrance both exciting and fun, just as writing this book has been. It's a good idea to reflect, remember, and journal all God has done. This is a wonderful exercise. Don't leave it to memory. Write down all the wonderful things God has done for you.

March 16

In prayer, the words *rise up* kept coming to the forefront of my mind. I also wrote about *rise up* in my Joel Osteen *50 Days with God* in the journal section. The next day, March 17, I got busy with something and didn't do my random Bible open. Here's what I wrote in my journal: "God didn't miss a beat with me even though I missed a day with him." I then did my random Bible opening. Lo and behold, I went to Judges 5:12: "Awake, awake, utter a song! Arise! Awake!"

March 17

In my journals I wrote: "It's time for me to *rise up* out of the ashes." Lo and behold, I prayed and did my random Bible opening right to Jonah 3:1–3:

> And the word of the Lord came to Jonah the second time saying Arise, go to Nineveh, that great city, and preach and cry out to it the preaching that I tell you. So, Jonah arose and went to Nineveh.

Interesting enough, Joni had just told me we were going to make it a three-day drive to go to Chandler, Arizona, where we were moving. Also, this was the second time that the word *rise* came to me in the last two days: "And the Lord came to Jonah the second time."

March 22

I prayed and asked God to share something special with me, and I did my random Bible opening. Lo and behold, it was Sunday, the Sabbath day, and I opened to Ezekiel 20:19:

> I the Lord am your God; walk in My statutes and keep My ordinances, and hallow (separate and keep holy) My Sabbaths, and they shall be a sign between Me and you, that you may know, understand, and realize that I am the Lord your God. (Ezekiel 20:19–20 AMP)

March 23

It took most of the previous day to read through all the God stories written in my miracle notebook. I wrote: "It's very obvious God is with me and showing me His power to prove the mission of this book that He is available and willing to perform miracles for us, even instant ones." I prayed and did my random Bible opening. Lo and behold, I opened to the beginning of the Song of Solomon where Joyce Meyer wrote: "Some people believe the Song of Solomon applies only to a physical love relationship while others believe it is entirely symbolic of God's love for his people. It reveals the passion which God loves us. It also reminds us that God is chasing us, wooing us, and pursuing us."

March 24

I prayed and asked God to heal a physical ailment. A few hours later this injury was healing remarkably fast. I prayed and asked God to show me something related to His healing on this day. I did my random Bible opening. Lo and behold, I opened to Daniel 4:2–3 (AMP):

It seemed good to me to show the signs and wonders
that the Most High God has performed toward me.
How great are His signs! And how mighty His wonders!

March 25
I was feeling down and discouraged about my financial situation
from a recently failed marriage and a failed business partnership. I
prayed and asked God to show me words of encouragement. I did
my random Bible opening. Lo and behold, I opened to Joel, which
is all about encouragement!

Fear not, O land; be glad and rejoice, for the lord
has done great things! (Joel 2:21 AMP)

Be glad then, you children of Zion, and rejoice in
the Lord, your God; for He gives you the former
or early rain in just measure and in righteousness,
and He causes to come down for you the rain, the
former rain and the latter rain, as before. (2:23)

And I will restore or replace for you the years that
the locust has eaten—the hopping locust, the
striping locust, and the crawling locust, My great
army which I sent among you. (2:25)

And you shall eat in plenty and be satisfied and
praise the name of the Lord, your God, Who has
dealt wondrously with you. And My people shall
never be put to shame. (2:26)

And afterward I will pour out My spirit upon
all flesh; and your sons and your daughters shall
prophesy, your old men shall dream dreams, your
young men shall see visions. (2:28)

> And whoever shall call on the name of the Lord
> shall be delivered and saved, for in Mount Zion
> and in Jerusalem there shall be those who escape,
> as the Lord has said, and among the remnant [of
> survivors] shall be those whom the Lord calls. (2:32)

Joyce says in *Putting the Word to Work*: "No matter how desperate your situation, God's promise is sure; He will save and deliver whoever calls upon him."

March 26

In my Joel Osteen's *50 Days to Better Living* journal, I wrote how discouraged I was with my financial situation. In fact, I told Joni: "I'm ready to throw everything in the *trash* and do something else with my life." Lo and behold, I opened to Jeremiah, where Joyce Meyer said: "You are chosen; God works with what the world would reject as useless and throws away as trash. Yet God chooses and uses what the world would reject!"

March 28

I woke up from a bad dream about my nasty divorce. I felt shame because of the way my relationships with my daughters ended during the divorce process. I felt afflicted with *shame* for my part in the tragedy of my broken relationships. I said a specific prayer for God to speak directly to my emotional wound. I then closed my eyes and flipped the Bible around in my hands multiple times. Lo and behold (Awesome!), I opened to Isaiah 54:1: "Sing O' Barren One." Then, in Joyce's commentary she writes (believe it or not): "Free from Shame." She goes on to say: "We know from Isaiah 54:4 that the Lord has promised to remove the shame and dishonor from us so that we remember it no more … you are healed from the pains and wounds of your past."

> Fear not, for you shall not be ashamed; neither be
> confounded and depressed, for you shall not be

put to shame. For you shall forget the shame of your youth, and you shall not [seriously] remember the reproach of your widowhood any more. (Isaiah 54:4 AMP)

March 29

I just finished an hour-long hike with Joni where I discussed all my bad choices in business and personal relationships. I came back and wrote about two pages in my journal about my "unwise choices of partners both in business and personally." Lo and behold, I prayed about this and then flipped the Bible all over the place in my hands and opened to 1 Kings: 6 where I read Joyce's commentary (believe it or not):

> Handling your relationships wisely: Solomon asked God for wisdom, and God gave it to him. Solomon wrote the Book of Proverbs, a collection of wise truths that have helped many people successfully live their day to day lives. I cannot overemphasize the importance of using wisdom as we deal with other people, family, friends, coworkers, neighbors, and even casual acquaintances. Ask God to give you wisdom in your relationships. He'll do it!

March 31

I had just finished reading from John Eldredge's book *Free to Live* on where the apostle Paul taught how Jesus changed all the rules and how Jesus is alive and his spirit dwells in each of us so we can be right, act right, and be righteous. Lo and behold, I prayed about this and flipped the Bible all over the place in my hands and opened to Galatians where the top of the page is Joyce's commentary: "How to handle God's call" where the first word I saw was *Paul*: "Paul said that he kept the news of his calling to himself; he did not check it out with the 'big guys' who were supposed to hear from God. He knew what God did to him on the road to Damascus. He knew that he was forever changed."

> Yet we know that a man is justified or reckoned righteous and is in right standing with God not by works of the Law, but [only] through faith and [absolute] reliance on and adherence to and trust in Jesus Christ. [Therefore] we [ourselves] have believed on Christ Jesus, in order to be justified by faith in Christ and not by works of the Law, because by keeping legal rituals and by works no human being can ever be justified [declared righteous and put in right standing with God]. (Galatians 2:16 AMP)

In summary, March was quite a month with God! There could be no doubt that He was teaching me wisdom each week through a long series of random Bible openings. Soon, God takes this spiritual adventure to a whole new level that's filled with spectacular supernatural events. Stay with me as this journey will have you in awe of God's power to perform stupendous miracles, amazing wonders, and outrageous visions.

CHAPTER THIRTEEN

Jesus Is the Way

Faith is to believe what you do not see; the reward for this faith is to see what you believe.

—St. Augustine

The end of April is the month when my super-miracle happened. I'm once again going to highlight some of my favorite supernatural events in April. I started off the month watching a Joel Osteen video about how God is pushing us, testing us, and trying to put us in a better place. Joel says not to resist change as God has something much bigger and better in store for us.

April 1:

I read a few pages in my miracle notebook where I wrote what Joyce Meyer had written about the prophet Jeremiah. Here's how Joyce describes his faith:

> Yes, Jeremiah had problems just as we do. When God saw Jeremiah, He did not see perfection, but He obviously did see someone with a right heart

who believed in Him. He saw in Jeremiah two main ingredients essential to pleasing God; faith in God, and a deep desire to please God. Jeremiah, despite criticism, unpopularity, and attacks against him, faithfully delivered God's message to the nation of Judah. By doing so, he honored God, demonstrated faith and courage, and chose obedience over his personal preferences.

On this day, I prayed out loud: "God, I love you, and I will follow Your desired direction for my life." I closed my eyes, flipped the Bible around in my hands and did my random Bible opening. Lo and behold, I opened directly to Jeremiah 11:20!

> But, O Lord of hosts, Who judges rightly and justly, Who tests the heart and the mind, let me see Your vengeance on them, for to You I have revealed and committed my cause [rolling it upon You].

Right underneath this Bible quote was Joyce Meyer's *Life Point:* "Every time God gives us a test; we can tell how far we have come and how far we still have to go by how we react in the test. Embrace your tests as opportunities for growth and development."

April 2

I decided to say a prayer of thanks to God for answering our prayer on getting Joni and I to Arizona. My random Bible opening took me to Nehemiah, where I saw Joyce Meyer's *Life Point*: "We stand confident that everything is going to work out for the best. We are not to assume that the Lord will intervene and take care of all our problems without our invitation."

April 5

It was Easter Sunday when I read in Joel Osteen's *2015 Devotional Calendar*: "He is not here; he has risen, just as he said" (Matthew 28:6 NIV). Joel goes on to say:

> Jesus has risen! That's what we celebrate today and every day! The cross is bare, and the tomb is empty. His victory over sin and death provides each of us with an opportunity to start over, make a fresh start, and a new beginning.

In the journal part of Joel's devotional calendar, I wrote, "Jesus predicting and then achieving His resurrection after three days in the grave was the single greatest act in the history of the world." Then I prayed: *Thank You Jesus for producing the greatest miracles ever after dying on the cross for my sin and saving my soul. Thank You for showing me all Your wondrous signs and for recognizing my heart and my love for You.*

Then, of course, I did my random Bible opening and came to Romans 1. Lo and behold (believe it or not), it's all about the Good News, the risen Christ!

> And declared to be the Son of God with power, according to the Spirit of holiness, by the resurrection from the dead. (Romans 1:4 NIV)

April 6

I read in Joel Osteen's *2015 Devotional Calendar*: "Take delight in the Lord, and He will give you the desires of your heart" (Psalm 37:4). I prayed, and Lo and behold, I opened to Jeremiah 36:1–2:

> In the 4th year … this word came from the Lord;
> Take a scroll for a book and write on it all the words
> I have spoken to you.

Reading this passage reflects my desire to write this book filled with all of God's words and all the miracles He performed.

April 11

I had just awakened from a vivid dream. It was about me being in the middle of a raging fire where God told me to stand. I was not afraid and felt 100 percent protected. I stood there as the fire blazed all around me, and all the time I was trusting in God's protection.

Lo and behold, it was just the day before that Joni and I had discussed "listening to vivid dreams from God." The timing of the dream was no accident. Interestingly, as I was writing in my black pen, it ran out of ink, and I was left with only a red pen that wrote like fire. I prayed and asked God to show me in a random Bible opening what the dream was about. Lo and behold, I opened to Jeremiah 20:9:

> If I say, I will not make mention of (the Lord) or speak any more in His name, in my mind and heart it is as if there was a burning fire shut up in my bones. And I am weary of endurance and holding it in; I cannot (contain it any longer).

In my miracle journal, I wrote the following in my red pen that made the words look on fire: "First of all, I'm no longer surprised at how this unique way of God communicating is all working out and how it worked again today! And today, of all days, after having had a powerful dream last night about fire. I'm still amazed, but no longer surprised, how perfectly God is orchestrating all these random Bible openings. Once again, God answered me perfectly and specifically to what happened, and He answered my prayer!" The Fire Dream, and the random Bible opening mentioning the word fire, were all written with my red fire pen. What an awesome God!

April 12

In my miracle journal I wrote this with my fire pen: "I won't get burned by life again because I'm putting God first in my life. Putting God as my number one priority is what life is all about. My temporary existence on this planet is utterly meaningless unless I build treasures in heaven and that means always loving God, having 100% faith in Him, and wanting to please Him by always coming to Him with a pure heart of love."

Lo and behold! I did my random Bible opening to the very beginning of Colossians, where I read Joyce Meyer's *Everyday Life Principles*: "In everything you do, Keep Jesus First." In her introduction to Colossians, she goes on to say: "Paul's message in his letter to the Colossians is all about Jesus. Among all the great teachings in Colossians, Paul continually urges us to keep Jesus first in our lives." She summarizes with; "I pray that you see Jesus in ways you never have before and that His presence and power will increase in your life."

In my journal I wrote: "In summary, put Jesus first as this is pleasing to God. I love the fact that once again God let me know, beyond a shadow of a doubt, that He will meet me in the present moment, precisely where my mind is at that moment, and at the exact moment of my prayer."

April 13

In my journal I wrote: "I had some concerns as I started on my new book (*God Stories: Answered Prayers and Instant Miracles*) as I was trying to prove God's power, but I believed! I received! God is behind it all!" I flipped the Bible around several times in my hands with my eyes closed after I prayed. Lo and behold, my random Bible opening: "The Lord says this to you; Be not afraid or be dismayed at this great multitude; for the battle is not yours, but God's (2 Chronicles 20:15 AMP).

After this random Bible opening, I wrote in my journal: "The bottom line is this; God will fight my battles ... He will heal me financially … He will restore my lost relationships with my daughters … and God will open up new doors. God has a plan, and He is in my life; He is number one in my life. I trust Him 100% with everything. God will fight and win battles upon my behalf."

> You shall not need to fight in this battle; take your positions, stand still, and see the deliverance of the Lord [Who is] with you, O Judah and Jerusalem. Fear not nor be dismayed. Tomorrow, go out against them, for the Lord is with you. (2 Chronicles 20:15–17)

> Joyce Meyer in her *Life Point*: "When we learn to seek God and wait on Him; He will answer us."

April 14

I had just finished reading the chapter on health in Brian Tracy's book *No Excuses!* Brian states: "Make it a goal to live to 80 or even 100 years old." He then asks: "What one thing would you do to live to 100?" I wrote down: "I will live in peace, joy, and love with 100% of my trust in God and Jesus." I prayed and then flipped the Bible all over the place with my eyes closed. Lo and behold, my random Bible opening took me to this perfect answer:

> My son, forget not my law or teaching, but let your heart keep my commandments; For length of days and years of a life [worth living] and tranquility [inward and outward and continuing through old age till death], these shall add to you. (Proverbs 3:1–2 AMP)

After I read this, I was filled with the joy of the Lord as the Holy Spirit covered my entire being because God continues to meet me right where I'm at each day, and in every moment that I pray to Him.

April 15

Joni had given me a new book to read by John Eldredge, *Walking with God*. I didn't feel like taking on a new book to read. I secretly put it back on her bookshelf. About a week later, she gave it back to me. I immediately knew this was a book I must read and do so carefully. Fortunately, I loved the book, and on page 28, John Eldredge asks an important question: "What is the life God wants you to live?" He then says; "If we can get an answer to that question; it will change everything." After reading this, I pondered the question and I prayed: *God, what path would You have me go?*

With my eyes closed, I did something unusual. I closed my eyes, and I really concentrated on where I felt God wanted me to open the Bible on this particular random Bible opening. Lo and behold, my random Bible opening took me to the very beginning of Psalms where Joyce Meyer writes: "The writers were very honest with God, and they communicated with Him from their hearts. My personal favorite is Psalm 27." I knew this was my direct answer from God to my prayer about my future path. Here it is: "Teach me Your way, O Lord, and lead me in a plain and even path because of my enemies [those who lie in wait for me] (Psalm 27:11 AMP).

Joyce sums it all up this way with the title: Seek the "one thing."

"Unfortunately, we get so distracted with the busy details of our lives that we neglect the most important thing; spending time with God. How foolish we are to spend our lives seeking those things that cannot satisfy while we ignore God, the 'one thing' who can give us great joy, peace, satisfaction, and contentment. The world is full of empty people who are trying to satisfy the void in their lives with a new car, a promotion at work, a human relationship, a vacation, or some other thing. Their efforts to find fulfillment in those things never work. If you put God first in everything you do, you will be so blessed." And here came my answer: "Investing your life in God is the very best thing you can do."

In my journal I wrote: "How will I do all this? By putting God behind everything I do and putting God as my number one priority in my life, and by walking with God every single day of my life, and by consulting with God on every major decision for my life. God will be my source of inspiration. Finally, I must trust God 100%. I have no one to fear as God has shown me, He is with me. The attacks by the enemy will fail as I'm keeping my peace by having complete trust in God. Jesus will use His power to heal me in *all* ways."

April 16

No sooner than I wrote, "the attacks by the enemy (Satan) will fail" and then ... I came under heavy assault that was targeted directly at my emotions. I wrote, "It's been a rough several years for me in so many different ways: a failed marriage, a failed business partnership, and broken relationships with my two beautiful daughters." After writing this, I hit a new low in my emotions, but I immediately recognized what was happening. The enemy was on full attack as I was pivoting my life to make a daily commitment to Christ in everything I do.

Satan attacked me where it hurt the most (my broken relationship with my two precious daughters), and he twisted those arrows deep inside my heart. I knew it was time to put on the full armor of God. I looked through my miracle notebook with words God spoke to me and the miracles He performed for me. Then, I quickly received relief from my emotional pain. The enemy's attack got a brief battle-win, but I got the victory in the war on my emotions. I prayed and did my random Bible opening. Lo and behold! I open to Esther 9:1: "The enemies had planned for a massacre; it was turned to the contrary."

Here is what I wrote in my journal:

> I never really got all the talk about the 'enemy' but now I get it! Out of nowhere I sank hard emotionally, and initially I had no idea what was going on. Then it came to me. I was under attack! Satan wants to destroy this new path I'm on with

God. This is very encouraging to me because it tells me I'm worth fighting for, meaning God has something excellent in store for me, and the enemy can smell it. He wanted to destroy and "massacre" me, but he lost—I turned to God's Word, and I read my miracle journal furiously, and I 'got it.' I prayed, and I felt all better. God's word is my armor against the evil one. God is with me—I know this. God is proving it to me just as I requested. Now, Satan wants to shake me up, and this is good news as it shows God is up to something, and the enemy is compelled to attack. It is awesome to know I'm worth fighting for!

April 17

No sooner than I believed that I had won the war, the enemy attacked again, but this time he went on full assault! I was reading Brian Tracy's book, *No Excuses!*, where "children" was the topic of discussion. Once again, the enemy attacked my sore spot of the broken relationships with my two precious daughters that resulted from the painful divorce process. The enemy twisted the arrow deeper into my heart as I wrote about my shame while answering all of Brian Tracy's questions about taking personal responsibility for everything in my life. The more I wrote, the more I felt like a complete failure. As I looked at the wreckage of my life, I cried out to God to answer me in this time of affliction. Then, I did my random Bible opening.

Lo and behold! Jesus had me open the Bible to Psalm 51, to the chief musician. A psalm of David, when Nathan the prophet came to him after he had sinned with Bathsheba.

Have Mercy upon me, O God, according to Your steadfast love; according to the multitude of Your tender mercy and loving kindness blot out my transgressions. (Psalm 51:1 AMP)

Wash me thoroughly [and repeatedly] from my iniquity and guilt and cleanse me and make me wholly pure from my sin! (51:2)

For I am conscious of my transgressions and I acknowledge them; my sin is ever before me. (51:3)

Against You, You only, have I sinned and done that which is evil in Your sight, so that You are justified in Your sentence and faultless in Your judgement. (51:4)

Behold, I was brought forth in [a state of] iniquity; my mother was sinful who conceived me [and I too am sinful]. (51:5)

Behold, You desire truth in the inner being; make me therefore to know wisdom in my inmost heart. (51:6)

Purify me with hyssop, and I shall be clean [ceremonially]; wash me, and I shall [in reality] be whiter than snow. (51:7)

Make me to hear joy and gladness and be satisfied; let the bones which You have broken rejoice. (51:8

Hide Your face from my sins and blot out all my guilt and iniquities. (51:9)

Create in me a clean heart, O God, and renew a right, persevering, and steadfast spirit within me. (51:10)

51:11 Cast me not away from Your presence and take not Your Holy Spirit from me.

51:12 Restore to me with joy of Your salvation and uphold me with a willing spirit.

Joyce Meyer says this in her *Life Point*:

> In Psalm 51, King David cries out to God for mercy and forgiveness because the Lord had been dealing with him about his sin with Bathsheba and the murder of her husband. Psalm 51:6 conveys a powerful message. It says that God desires truth in the inner being. That means if we want to receive God's blessings, we must be honest with Him about our sins and ourselves. Let me encourage you not to let sin linger in your life. We all sin, and when we do, we need to be quick to repent.

Here is what I wrote in my miracle journal: "Behold, the Lord just confirmed my new clean heart. Today's random Bible opening was perfect and exactly what I needed to read, and I feel blessed and washed clean from *all* my past shame—God is my deliverer!"

Jesus Is the Way

April 19

It was Sunday, the Sabbath day, where I was going to attend a meeting with a small home group called The Way International. I asked God to show me something about The Way. I closed my eyes and flipped the Bible around and did my random Bible opening. Lo and behold, my eyes immediately go to Acts 9:2, and one of the very first words I read was *the way*! And in fact, I saw *the way* multiple times in Acts 9:1–27:

Meanwhile Saul, still drawing his breath hard from threatening and murderous desire against the disciples of the Lord, went to the high priest. (9:1)

And requested of him letters to the synagogues at Damascus [authorizing him], so that if he found any men or women belonging to the Way [of life as determined by faith in Jesus Christ], he might bring them bound [with chains] to Jerusalem. (9:2)

Now as he traveled on, he came near to Damascus, and suddenly a light from heaven flashed around him, (9:3)

And he fell to the ground. Then he heard a voice saying to him, Saul, Saul, why are you persecuting [harassing, troubling, and molesting] Me? (9:4)

And Saul said, Who are You, Lord? And He said, I am Jesus, Whom you are persecuting. (9:5)

Trembling and astonished he asked, "Lord, what do You desire me to do"? The Lord said to him, "But arise and go into the city, and you will be told what you must do." (9:6)

The men who were accompanying him were unable to speak, hearing the voice but seeing no one. (9:7)

Then Saul got up from the ground, but though his eyes were opened, he could not see anything; so, they led him by the hand and brought him into Damascus. (9:8)

And he was unable to see for three days, and neither ate nor drank [anything]. (9:9)

Now there was in Damascus a disciple named Ananias. The Lord said to him in a vision, Ananias, and he answered, Here am I, Lord. (9:10)

And the Lord said to him; Get up and go to the street called Straight and ask at the house of Judas for a man of Tarsus named Saul, for behold, he is praying [there]. (9:11)

And he has seen in a vision a man named Ananias enter and lay his hands on him so that he might regain his sight. (9:12)

But Ananias answered, Lord; I have heard many people tell about this man, especially how much evil and what great suffering he has brought on Your saints at Jerusalem. (9:13)

Now he is here and has authority from the high priests to put in chains all who call upon Your name. (9:14)

But the Lord said to him, Go, for this man is a chosen instrument of Mine to bear My name before the Gentiles and kings and the descendants of Israel; (9:15)

For I will make clear to him how much he will be afflicted and must endure and suffer for My name's sake. (9:16)

So Ananias left and went into the house. And he laid his hands on Saul and said, Brother Saul, the Lord

Jesus, Who appeared to you along the way by which you came here, has sent me that you may recover your sight and be filled with the Holy Spirit. (9:17)

And instantly something like scales fell from [Saul's] eyes, and he recovered his sight. Then he arose and was baptized. (9:18)

And after he took some food, he was strengthened. For several days [afterward] he remained with the disciples at Damascus. (9:19)

And immediately in the synagogues he proclaimed Jesus, saying, He is the Son of God! (9:20)

And all who heard him were amazed and said, Is not this the very man who harassed and overthrew and destroyed in Jerusalem those who called upon this Name? And he has come here for the express purpose of arresting them and bringing them in chains before the chief priests. (9:21)

But Saul increased all the more in strength, and continued to confound and put confusion to the Jews who lived in Damascus by comparing and examining evidence and proving that Jesus is the Christ (the Messiah). (9:22)

After considerable time had elapsed, the Jews conspired to put Saul out of the way by slaying him. (9:23)

But [the knowledge of] their plot was made known to Saul. They were guarding the [city's] gates day and night to kill him. (9:24)

But his disciples took him at night and let him down through the [city's] wall, lowering him in a basket or hamper. (9:25)

And when he had arrived in Jerusalem, he tried to associate himself with the disciples; but they were all afraid of him, for they did not believe he really was a disciple. (9:26)

However, Barnabas took him and brought him to the apostles, and he explained to them how along the way he had seen the Lord, Who spoke to him, and how at Damascus he had preached freely and confidently and courageously in the name of Jesus. (9:27)

Later, after The Way International group meeting, I was sitting in the living room relaxing. I looked at the Bible my daughter Grace had given me on my birthday on March 8, 2001. I wrote a little note in the Bible and put it back on the table. Suddenly, I felt this strong urge to pick it up and do my random Bible opening. At first, I hesitated as this was not part of the daily routine. I only do one random opening after a prayer inside my Hour of Spiritual Power. Lo and behold, the very first words I read on the random Bible opening: "John the Baptist Prepares the Way."

And then further, Mark 1:2–3 (NIV): "I will send my messenger ahead of you, who will prepare your way—a voice of one calling in the desert, 'Prepare the way for the Lord, make straight paths for him.'" By the way (pun intended), I met Kathe Everson at The Way gathering in her home, and she's the person who kindly did the first edits for this book.

April 21

I was on the outside deck praying to God for new miracles to be manifested in my life. I said a prayer, closed my eyes, and did my random Bible opening. My eyes went to Mark 11:24: "For this reason I am telling you, whatever you ask for in prayer, believe that it is granted you, and you will."

April 22

I drank too much hard alcohol the night before, and I felt bad about it. I then prayed to God for self-control and self-mastery. I finished the prayer by asking God: *Is wine okay?* After I said this specific prayer, with my eyes closed, I did my random Bible opening. Lo and behold, my eyes went to Song of Solomon 7:9 where I read specifically about wine, and also fruit and vineyards were all over the page!

> And your kisses like the best wine that goes down smoothly and sweetly for my beloved gliding over his lips while he sleeps! (Song of Solomon 7:9 AMP)

April 23

As I read Joel Osteen's *Today's Word Devotional Calendar*, I circled the word *stronghold*. Then, I was reading *Walking with God*, and the only word I circled was *strong* man. For some reason, the word *strong* was my word from God that day, and I knew it. I got on my knees and said a prayer about the word *strong*. I then did my random Bible opening.

Lo and behold! My eyes went to Joyce's commentary on page 353 in the *Everyday Life Bible* where she says to be *strong* in God:

> Joshua fought many battles in order to finally enter the Promised Land. As the Lord gave him direction all along the way, He repeatedly told him to be of good courage. Courage means having a good attitude in the face of dangerous or frightening circumstances. The same is true of our daily walk. When you are tempted to lose courage, remember

that the joy of the Lord is your strength. Like Joshua, all of your enemies will be utterly defeated as you stay strong in God.

Joshua said to them, Fear not, nor be dismayed; be strong and of good courage. For thus shall the Lord do to all your enemies against whom you fight. (Joshua 10:25 AMP)

In summary, it is plain to see God was granting me wisdom through His Word, just as I had asked for in my prayers. He did it through random Bible openings in the Joyce Meyer *Everyday Life Bible*. For believers, the Bible is where the greatest of all spiritual wisdom exists. In the next chapter, I will tell you about the most amazing night of my life and the incredible supernatural events that followed.

CHAPTER FOURTEEN

God Shows Signs and Wonders

For the vision is yet for an appointed time and it hastens to the end [fulfillment]; it will not deceive or disappoint. Though it tarry, wait [earnestly] for it, because it will surely come; it will not be behindhand on its appointed day.

—Habakkuk 2:3 AMP

And afterward I will pour out My Spirit upon all flesh; and your sons and your daughters shall prophesy, your old men shall dream dreams, your young men shall see visions.

—Joel 2:28 AMP

This next God story is one the most amazing experiences of my life. It happened one evening when I was home alone at my apartment. I had been debating about whether I should write this book. I had my doubts because I didn't feel qualified to write about my Lord and Savior Jesus Christ. However, I knew the Lord wanted me to reveal all the miracles He performed in my life by writing them in a book.

I decided to sit, think, and pray on the deck of my apartment as it was a beautiful night in Chandler, Arizona. I moved the two deck chairs that faced the apartment, and I turned them around to face the sky. As I sat on the deck thinking about writing this book, I saw something that caught my attention. A light was moving wildly in the sky. At first, I thought it was a falling star, but it was moving rapidly, and in every direction. As I stood up and looked more closely, the light started to move even more spastically. For some reason, I felt like this light was trying to get my attention.

As I watched this strange light show in the sky, I leaned over the railing of the deck to see if anybody else was around. I wanted to bring someone's attention to this frantic light movement in the sky. I didn't see anyone walking below, so I decided to look for my iPhone to turn on the video capability. As I reached for my cell, I was so fascinated that I couldn't take my eyes off the wild light show. However, I briefly looked down to get the video all set up on my cell phone when at the exact moment I looked up, the light suddenly hid behind a gigantic cloud. I stood there with my iPhone for about five minutes hoping the spastic light would come back out from behind the cloud. At the time, I thought the spastic light was some kind of UFO.

As I looked up, I noticed how strange it was that the illuminated light was trapped behind an abnormally large cloud on a clear night sky. After a while, I finally gave up any hope that the wild light was coming out from behind that enormous cloud. I went back inside my apartment filled with amazement, but I was sad about the light not coming back out from behind the cloud.

A few minutes later, I wondered if that frantic light was a sign from God. I had been thinking about Him when I saw the light rapidly moving in multiple directions in the sky. It was a long shot, but given all the past miracles in my life, it certainly seemed like a real possibility that this light show was indeed a sign from God. As

I sat inside the apartment, I got the Bible in my hands and prayed: *Heavenly Father, if that was a sign from You tonight, I ask that You confirm it with me in a random Bible opening. If I see no confirmation, I will know the light show was not sent from You. Amen.*

When I opened the Bible with my eyes closed, God sent me to Numbers. I started reading with great hope and anticipation of seeing some confirmation, but instead all I read was God instructing Moses on numbering the tribes of Israel. I read both pages that I randomly opened to, but there wasn't any confirmation I could see that God sent me the amazing light show in the sky. As you might expect, I was extremely disappointed. As I closed the Bible, I figured I had just seen a UFO. But then, I prayed: *Lord, that's not like You to show me absolutely nothing on a random Bible opening?*

Lo and behold, in my heart I heard: **Go back to the beginning**. I immediately went back to my Bible and reopened to the beginning of Numbers where I read the introduction to Numbers in my Joyce Meyer *Everyday Life Bible* where she writes: "One of the primary themes in Numbers is God's guidance. God made His leading clear in the appearance of a cloud."

My entire body suddenly erupted with power from the Holy Spirit! God fantastically confirmed His holy presence not only on the inside of my body, but the Holy Spirit surrounded my entire body, and it seemed to my senses that the presence of the Lord filled the apartment. Once this new revelation entered my mind, I uttered out loud; "I was focused on the spastic light when You were the cloud!"

With great excitement, I ran outside to see the cloud, which I believed to be the presence of God right before my very eyes! Even though it was only a few minutes later, the sky was clear except for one teeny-tiny cloud far away in the distance, and within seconds, it disappeared. I was still full of excitement as I walked back inside the apartment to read more about God's appearance to His people as a cloud in Numbers.

After a couple minutes of reading, I stopped because I was

disappointed in myself. I realized that my lack of Bible knowledge had me focused on the wild spastic light when God had just showed me His presence in the form of a cloud. I was in awe that God had appeared to me in the form of a gigantic cloud that covered much of the clear night sky. My awe of God only intensified when He immediately confirmed it was Him when the Holy Spirit directed my random Bible opening to Numbers. I decided to go back outside for one more look for the giant cloud, but instead all I saw was a clear sky filled with stars.

Lo and behold, I had another vision! Right where the cloud had been, there appeared another strange and rather large figure. At first, I thought it was an airplane, but it was multiple times larger and faster than a plane. In fact, it looked like a giant prehistoric bird! But this was no ordinary bird as it appeared to have dozens of large doves that fit perfectly inside its rather large prehistoric bodily structure. The giant bird also appeared to have a fire burning inside its belly!

As the giant prehistoric-looking bird flew very slowly from the far left to right in front of me, I immediately leaned over the balcony looking for another person to have them see the giant figure in the sky. But once again, no one was around. My next thought was to grab my iPhone and videotape the outrageous-looking figure. As it was flying gracefully from left to the right of me, I fumbled around trying to grab the cell phone without taking my eyes off the Fire Bird. Suddenly, it started to pick up speed, and by the time I got my iPhone in my hand with the video option ready to go, the Great Fire Bird completely disappeared in the night sky right in front of my eyes!

After this supernatural event, I was absolutely blown away by this entire experience. In fact, I was in a state of shock knowing in my heart that I had just witnessed the manifestation of God as an enormous cloud and again as a Great Fire Bird! These supernatural events had me back in my apartment reading more in Numbers where apparently God not only appeared as a cloud, but he also appeared to Moses and the Israelites as fire. My first thought was maybe God appeared to me as both a cloud and fire but with the fire being inside the belly of this prehistoric-looking creature. Maybe God answered my disappointment of the disappearing cloud by giving me this powerful vision.

The next day when Joni came home from her business trip, I told her the entire story. She said I had a vision from God and that "visons are extremely rare and very significant." She fully understood the cloud but she was much more intrigued about the prehistoric-looking Fire Bird. Joni also said that this vision would reveal itself by God at some future point in time. She is a well-educated Christian woman who has taken many sophisticated studies on the Word. I believed what she said, but I couldn't help but wonder how in the world a prehistoric bird could ever appear in my life again, let alone in a way that would confirm this incredible vision. In the next chapter, I'm going to share with you how God eventually revealed it all to me.

God Is Gracious

Not too long after my incredible vision, I received a phone call that my dad was back in the hospital. I immediately called his doctor, who said, "I'm sorry, but that cancer has returned and it's spreading fast, and he doesn't have long. In fact, he will likely be gone by the end of the day but almost certainly by tomorrow morning." It sounded hopeless that I would ever see my dad alive again because I was in Arizona and he was in New York. Early the next morning, I called the hospital before I got on my flight to New York. Dad was still breathing but barely alive. I had many people praying for me that he would hang on until I got to his bedside.

Lo and behold, I arrived at the hospital around 9:00 p.m. and my Dad was still alive, but he was in a deep coma. Instead of telling you the whole story, I'm simply going to share several texts to my mom. Please know as you read these texts, my dad could not speak or move any part of his body.

May 22, 2015: Just spoke to Dad's doctor. He said it's possible that he makes it until tomorrow but unlikely as he believes Dad will be gone by day's end. I'm getting a ticket back East ASAP. My friend Devin has free miles for me. Sent from my iPhone.

Dad was in a coma but still alive when I arrived Saturday night. Sent from my iPhone.

Dad woke up from his coma, but he cannot move or talk, but he seems aware of everything. Sent from my iPhone.

I got several small, attempted smiles on Dad's face. Sent from my iPhone.

I'm here in the room with my dad laying hands on him and praying over him. Doing what I can to make him comfortable by cooling him off with cool rags. He has been trying to smile in his final hours. Sent from my iPhone.

I anointed his head and body with my best cologne. He really liked that. Sent from my iPhone.

To recognize his Mohawk Indian heritage; I painted him up with baby powder as his war paint; he liked that a lot. Sent from my iPhone.

He is such a strong man, my hero. Sent from my iPhone.

We now have Roy Orbison, his favorite artist, playing for him in the room. Sent from my iPhone.

Several people texted me and asked how I was doing; I responded: I'm emotionally raw and physically exhausted so I'm going to bed now as we are all so wiped out from a long day. But I will be checking up on him throughout the night. He is wide awake and breathing well, and he seems comfortable. Sent from my iPhone.

Still no change; the nurse gave him a small dose of anti-anxiety medicine (Ativan) so he would settle down through this ordeal as the morphine has him hyped-up right now. But because of the Ativan, he finally got to sleep around midnight and is still sleeping, which we believe he needed after a big deal of multiple visitors and phone calls saying final goodbyes to Dad. His body is gone, but he continues to be a Mohawk warrior putting up a big fight. Sent from my iPhone.

This morning Dad woke up. I ministered to him claiming God's promises from the Word. I told him I was taking the Indian paint off his body because this battle is no longer worth fighting. As I wiped off the powder (war paint), I told him that we understood he was not being "stubborn" (as the nurse had suggested) but that he was just obeying his very nature and fighting as any great Indian warrior would fight in an unwanted battle.

I told him it was time to put the Mohawk aside and to let this process unfold but in great confidence that his spiritual-body would emerge from his pain-body the way a beautiful butterfly emerges from its cocoon. He seemed to quietly settle down, and slowly he got more peaceful. I think he is truly starting to let go from the pain and suffering. He squeezed his eyes tightly for a few seconds and then reopened them for all of us as that's his sign of I Love You that we established together a couple days ago. I believe today is the day, but that's between him and the Lord. Sent from my iPhone.

He has put up yet another good fight, but this long-fought battle with cancer is now coming to the very end. I'm supremely confident his end is simply a new beginning as he transitions from the physical world to the spiritual world. I told him that we loved him, as so many do and have shown him in recent days. I also told him that we would see him again on the other side in "paradise" as promised on the Cross. We all cried this morning. Thanks for all your thoughts and prayers. Sent from my iPhone.

After falling back into a sleep coma for two days, Dad woke up, but he did not comprehend I was there. He dropped back off as I looked into his eyes rolling to the back of his head. Seeing him like this is horrible, but the truth is that death is a natural part of this thing we call the human experience. Sent from my iPhone.

My step-grandma Kathy has one plot next to grandma and grandpa, and she said we could have the plot for my dad and for free! I was so happy that I broke down in tears and cried on my stepmom's shoulder in the hospital room today. Sent from my iPhone.

I went to the burial site with my stepbrother Rodney, where

I immediately broke down in tears. My step-grandmother was kind enough to give my dad the plot next to Dad's mother and grandmother. He will be buried near my grandma & grandpa Finkle and my great-grandmother Marcell. Sent from my iPhone.

Here's the text exchange between my mom and me on Friday afternoon May 29, 2015, the day before my dad died:

Text from my mom: How are things going? I have a feeling Dad will go to heaven tonight. I've shed a lot of tears today. His suffering will be over soon. Give him a hug from me.

Sent from iPhone.

My text: Mom, I read your text right after I had finished praying for God to please take Dad by morning. Sent from my iPhone.

May 30, 2015: My dad died, and he was a navy veteran. I went to a veterans memorial park to think and pray.

Saturday May 30, 2015: My cell phone text to my friends and family:

To everyone who loved my dad; this morning a wonderful man left this earth, his name was Ronald Anthony Coby. He was an outstanding father and a loving husband. His doctor told me eight days ago while I was on the West Coast that he was "sorry" but that my father would be deceased before I could arrive and likely "by the end of the day."

Several people prayed that my dad would hold on until his only son arrived to pay his final respects. Upon arriving at the hospital, my dad was in a sleep-coma. However, the next day he woke up. Even though he could not lift his arms or speak a word, he was fully aware and communicated to all of us in the room with his facial expressions.

It was my honor to pray over him and to send him off with the highest respect I could possibly think of. In honor of his Mohawk heritage, I painted him up in baby powder, which I made to look like war paint. I told my dad he had been a brave warrior throughout his long battle with cancer. He really liked that and responded in what were several attempted smiles. Then, I anointed his head and body with my best cologne. He also liked that, and he took several deep breaths. The smell of decay coming off his broken and sweaty body was temporarily replaced with a sweet-smelling fragrance from my cologne.

I looked deep into my father's eyes as he locked squarely unto mine as I assured him he was to leave his physical pain-body and that his spiritual pain-free body would soon see the Light of God. I expressed excitement in that image, and he once again gave me several attempted smiles. I told him of a couple incredible miracles that had manifested in my life, and he was finally able to temporarily put a full smile on his face. I could see pure amazement in his eyes. These were all beautiful and touching moments—ones I will never forget.

I made sure everyone could say their final goodbyes over the phone to him by holding the phone to his ear. Each phone call had him moved, and that was clearly expressed through his body's movement and in the rapid movement of his eyebrows. Others had me express their love for him personally and for each person I did, he showed me his emotions by raising his eyebrows. We established "I Love You" by him closing his eyes tightly for a few seconds. And in fact, that was the very last eye contact we had together.

Dad's morphine levels had to be slowly increased until he was no longer coherent or aware in his last couple days. Before that, I slept at the hospital for five nights. It was not easy to hear him groan in discomfort throughout the night and then seeing the clear deterioration in the morning. Sadly, it's a vision I will never forget, but it was also a wonderful blessing to have ministered to him in his last state of awareness.

Due to a series of unusual events, God spared me from having to see my dad breathe his very last breath. I'm so grateful for that because God wanted my last vision to be of my dad squinting his eyes with me knowing he was trying to say goodbye, and *Ronnie, I Love you* and then with me squinting back and saying to him; *I love you too, Dad*. That was our final goodbye to each other.

My stepbrothers and I did a toast for my dad at his house, but before we did; I played the saved voicemail from last year when God granted my dad a "remission-miracle" of perfect health for two months. The boys and I listened to the saved voice message of my dad in great health and happiness, and then we did a toast in honor of him. Afterwards, we all went back to the hospital room. I shared that story with my dad, and he gave me his fullest smile as I told him about the toast to him on the bridge where he loved to sit with his wife. Then, I played him the voice message he had left me. It was awesome to see the joy expressed on his face.

As I type, I'm praying with a thankful heart and sitting next to a veterans memorial park with the Bible and his mom's favorite book (*The Life of Christ*). In his hospital bed, my dad had the Bible under one hand and my grandma's favorite book under the other hand. Even though my dad suffered, he showed what a fighter and a lover he was. Dad was a warrior, and he fought a good fight, and that fighting spirit allowed so many of us to express our love for such a good-hearted man in his final hours.

In summary, for my part, it was a blessing to see my dad, the positive thinker, smiling in joy even amid great discomfort and pain. Late yesterday afternoon my mom texted me that she felt the Lord would take Dad by morning. I texted my mom back to tell her I had literally just asked God in a sincere prayer to take him by morning. God apparently listened, and He relieved my dad's pain and suffering this morning. Cancer is a horrible thing. What my dad went through is not something anyone should endure yet great blessings came out of his intense suffering. For believers like me, the story of suffering and glory is the story of the cross of Christ. I will miss my dad, but I know we will see each other again on the other side. Thanks for all your thoughts, prayers, and emotional support. Ronnie. Sent from my iPhone.

My final text to everyone on Friday June 5, 2015: Today was my dad's burial. They say that you never truly appreciate the sacrifices a parent has made for you until you become a parent yourself. I believe that is true. I can also say that you never fully appreciate someone you love until they are gone from your life. Today, I got full appreciation of the relationship I had with my dad as I watched a navy burial in honor of him. I also fully appreciated my dad in the multitude of memories that have flashed across my mind.

Despite the natural sadness that comes from the death of someone you love so dearly, I feel grateful for so many things. This gladness, inside my deep sadness, stems from the wonderful times I got to spend with my dad in life and in his last days of full awareness and consciousness. He was an excellent father, and I was lucky to have been brought up in a loving home. He coached me in baseball and soccer. He was my best-man at my wedding, and I got to be best man at his second wedding. He gave me great advice throughout my life, and what made it so great was that his intent was backed by love for his only son.

Only once did we ever have a problem between us, but within a few weeks, we worked through it because we both asked the same question: What's important here? We both came up with the same answer the exact same day. The answer: There is little that's more important in this world than meaningful loving relationships, especially between a parent and a child. On our makeup call, we spoke for over three hours, and our relationship became closer than ever from that day forward. I learned that in any meaningful relationship, love and respect are the only things needed to enable forgiveness and complete restoration. I also learned that false perceptions could destroy meaningful relationships until truth surfaces and mutual understanding erases all false realities that get created in conflict.

In his fight against cancer, Dad kept an excellent attitude. He fought many hard battles and had some successes along the way, but in the end, he lost the long war against cancer. My dad used to say many times to me; "Ronnie, never take your health for granted." He was right because life in poor health was like hell on earth for him, especially in his final week.

I'm left with wonderful memories of my dad in total health, and even in extreme difficulty, and even now in his death. In the end, I'd say that we passed the ultimate test of love and respect between a parent and a child.

In summary, I know that even in extreme difficulties, life is a gift to be cherished each day and that even in the most extreme of difficulties, blessings can be manifested. None of us know when we will die, but we know it's coming, and we should not believe that it's somewhere far into the future.

My dad lived in near perfect health his entire life until one day cancer changed his life forever. I will again say Dad was right about his words on health, and I'll add this: Never take your special relationships for granted, and always know that in the very end, love from meaningful relationships and the love of God are all that will matter. As everyone that knew my Dad would agree, he lived a life of love, and I can tell you he also had a sincere faith in God.

I know the essence of him left this earth as a soul filled with great love and pure faith. Therefore, I can feel some sense of joy even as I experience extreme sadness because I know his spirit returned to the ultimate source of love, which is God. To all of you that showed me love and support, I say thank you from the bottom of my heart. God Bless. Sent from my iPhone.

God Confirms His Miracles

Behold, God, my salvation! I will trust and not be afraid, for the Lord God is my strength and song; yes, He has become my salvation. (Isaiah 12:2 AMP)

As my dad was lying in his hospital bed just a few days before he passed, I walked outside to a quiet little park in front of the hospital. I was thinking about my dad lying on his deathbed when suddenly I saw some beautiful lilac bushes. I clipped a few of the strong-smelling purple flowers and brought them up to my dad's hospital room. When I put the pretty flowers up to his nose, he took several deep breaths. It was obvious he really liked the beautiful smell as those fragrant flowers were in total contrast to the smell of my father's sweaty body where the cancer was spreading.

After a few hours, I needed a break and went back down to the little park in front of the hospital. As I walked around, I saw an image on the ground of a dove that looked exactly like the doves in my vision. In the vision, there were dozens of doves all symmetrically aligned inside the body of The Great Fire Bird just as the picture of the dove painted on the ground at the hospital park. In my heart, I knew in the second that I saw the dove that this was a confirmation of my vision from God only a few weeks earlier.

God Is Awesome

The very next day, my stepbrother and I went to the burial site of where my dad would be in the plot next to his mother, his stepfather, and his grandmother. When I looked upon the grave site of my grandparents, I started to cry. I was filled with tears of both joy and sorrow. Joy of where my dad would be buried and sorrow knowing my dad would soon be buried. My stepbrother and I embraced as we cried together.

Lo and behold, I saw a giant, gawky-looking bird flying directly above us. I stopped crying as I knew immediately that this bird was from my vision of the Great Fire Bird in the sky. I said to my stepbrother: "look at that prehistoric-looking bird in the sky! What is it?" He responded, "I don't know, but my brothers and I call it the Snake Bird." I grabbed my iPhone to photograph the wild-looking bird, which I believe was a double-crested cormorant. I went to take a picture of the crazy looking bird, but right as I reached for my cell phone, it flew behind a forest of trees and out of sight. In the moment I saw that funky-looking creature fly over my head at the cemetery, I knew God was confirming the vision I had of Him as the Great Fire Bird in the Sky. But why? What did it all mean exactly?

Here's what I believe. First, God gave me the vision on the deck of my apartment as confirmation to write this book. Maybe God wanted to give me an incredible ending to this chapter, but He certainly wanted to let me know He was with me during the tragic loss of my father. Next, I believe when I heard a *still small voice* say **Go back to the beginning**, that God wanted me to hear His voice clearly and audibly for specific confirmation that my vision was indeed from Him. Also, I shared the incredible supernatural visions from God with my father in his final hours of consciousness. I could see in his facial expressions that he was filled with astonishment and wonder. His eyes displayed such amazement as I told him about the Great Fire Bird in the Arizona night sky. I also believe that sharing my vision from God gave my dad additional courage in his final hours on earth. Finally, I believe the Fire Bird Vision was a spiritual gift from God to me, and more importantly, it became a gift of comfort to my dad before he died.

CHAPTER FIFTEEN

Trust God

And Jesus answered him, The first of all the commandments is, Hear, O Israel; The Lord our God is one Lord: And thou shalt love the Lord thy God with all thy heart, and with all thy soul, and with all thy mind, and with all thy strength: this is the first commandment. And the second is like, namely this, thou shalt love thy neighbor as thyself. There is none other commandment greater than these.

—Mark 12:29–31 KJV

In the final chapter, I need to make a confession. When I finished chapter 14, I found myself asking this question: Why hasn't God answered my most desired prayer? I wondered how I could have confidence in ever speaking about what's been written in this book when my most heartfelt prayer, reconciliation with my two daughters, had not been answered. My relationships with Anna and Grace were destroyed shortly after their mom and I separated. My extreme sadness about this unanswered prayer resulted in me oftentimes feeling depressed and distanced from God. This extreme sadness hardened me, and the inner joy I felt writing this book slowly faded away.

I know many Christians would say the enemy, Satan, went on the attack, and maybe that's exactly what happened. What I know for sure is that I let my disappointment get the best of me, and instead of trusting God, I couldn't help but question why my biggest prayer was not being answered. This nagging sense of confusion and frustration left me feeling hollow inside. Once again, I felt shame extreme sadness from missing my two beautiful daughters. The loss of our once close father-daughter relationship wreaked havoc on my mind. I started to make new mistakes in my life, which left me feeling insecure about my future. Finally, a couple years went by, and everything came crashing down on me yet again.

It was the summer of 2017, and after six long years, I still had no relationship with my daughters. During these painful years of no communication, I would often find myself having the same vivid dream. In the dream, I would be embracing my two daughters in a joyful moment of reconciliation where I was filled with extreme happiness. Then, I would wake-up to reality, and my tears of joy would turn into tears of sadness. This repetitive dream would often leave me shaken for several days. In a better frame of mind, and stronger faith, I would have interpreted this dream as a vision from God. Instead, I felt sorry for myself, which left me feeling the pain of separation and a sense of injustice.

Also, in 2017, I found myself down to my last penny again where my final legitimate job opportunity in the financial industry turned into a total bust. The new fear of homelessness entered my mind as I was dead-broke, and rent was due in just four days. After my last hopeful attempt for a job didn't materialize, I was shaken to my core. In tears of despair, I dropped to my knees in a heartfelt prayer. I begged God for forgiveness, and once again, I did the thing that always saved me in the past. I prayed for a miracle.

Another Instant Miracle!

Lo and behold, about ten minutes later, I'm on the phone with a friend I had not spoken to for quite some time. Tom Hice sensed something was wrong, and he asked me: "What's going on, Ronnie, do you need some money?" Next thing I know, Tom was wiring the money I needed to pay rent, and he even sent an extra $100. Unbelievable! This was yet another answered prayer and instant miracle in my time of desperation.

A couple hours later, I had a strong impression to call a former business associate. Gene was someone who I had not talked to for several years. I decided to call, and Gene was thrilled to hear from me. He jokingly asked if I was "living under a rock" because he said none of our past mutual acquaintances knew where I was located. He informed me that he had a job opportunity and asked me to drive to Portland for a formal job interview with his boss. Lo and behold, only two days later, I had a nice-paying job along with five thousand dollars wired into my bank account. This was another perfectly answered prayer!

The job that I took led to many more amazing miracles where God sent me on a new adventure filled with an unbelievable series of events. As you know, I have mentioned several times throughout the book about the lost relationship and the separation from my two lovely daughters. You might recall in chapter 6 that I wrote the following:

I simply listed in my journal some other wonderful things God did for me, and I also listed some future miracles I desire in my life. One miracle request in particular looks nearly impossible, and that's the repair of the broken relationship with my two daughters after their mom and I divorced. It will likely take a long time for this seemingly improbable miracle to manifest, but I believe "with God all things are possible," and I believe in God's perfect timing. This prayed-for-miracle looks unlikely, but over time, one year or ten years, this seemingly impossible miracle will eventually become a reality.

God Works in Mysterious Ways

It was the summer of 2019 about one o'clock in the morning when I was awakened by a phone call. I didn't recognize the number and let the call go to my voice mail. When I listened to the message, it was from my daughter Grace. When I heard her voice, I immediately knew something was wrong. In her message she said my son Joseph was brutally attacked and that he was in the hospital getting surgery. My heart sank, and I was filled with dread. I called Grace right back, but every attempt went to her voice mail. My immediate response was to grab some clothes, hop in my car, and drive to see my son. This was a twenty-one-hour drive from Arizona to Idaho.

I was driving on just a few hours of sleep but with plenty of adrenaline to keep me awake. Finally, a few hours later, Grace and I connected. She told me that Joe was just getting out of surgery. Several hours later, I was pulled over by a policeman who told me I was driving twenty-plus miles per hour over the speed limit. He could see I was exhausted and a complete mess before asking me what was wrong. I told him the story about my son, and he was kind, and he took pity on me. He went back to his police car and wrote out directions for me because I was so delirious that I was actually driving in the wrong direction. He advised me to stop at the next hotel and drive to Idaho in the morning.

Even though I was only five hours away, I took his advice. He was an extremely nice policeman, and he didn't give me a ticket. He also made sure I got turned around and headed in the right direction. The next morning, I went to see my son. Even though he was beat in the head with a baseball bat multiple times by his surprise attacker, he was able to be released from the hospital. He needed surgery on his mangled hand and he had to get staples in his head, but other than a couple missing teeth, and being shaken up emotionally, he was going to be just fine.

God's Perfect Timing

My son texted me the address of his best friend's apartment where he was resting after surgery. He asked me to text him when I was a few minutes away. When I got out of the car, Joe was there waiting for me. He and I ran to each other and fiercely embraced. Tears wept down our faces as we each realized the dire consequences had Joe not been able to fight off his attacker. As we were embracing, his mom and my two daughters just happened to pull up! My heart sank when I saw my daughters for the first time in several years. They each gave me a cautious hug and said, "Hi, Dad."

I won't go into all the gory details, but my ex-wife, my two daughters, my son Joseph, and his best buddy, Andre, were all in the same room together. I noticed my daughters carefully observed as my ex-wife and I embraced and eventually exchanged kind words. We made peace in that moment as we were both grateful that our son was alive. This unusual reunion led to a few laughs as some fun family memories were being shared by Anna, Grace, and Joseph. It was clear to me that God turned this horrible attack on my son into an opportunity for reconciliation with my daughters.

I had no idea the incredible journey God was going to take me on during the several years of writing this book. The miracles He performed were amazing, and tears are running down my face as I type. God showed His power, His love, and His mercy to a flawed man, and I'm humbled to my core with a thankful heart. This journey with God, as written in this book, is basically the summary of my life with Him, my love for Him, and my belief in Him and His Son, Jesus Christ. The miracles, visions, and lessons from Jesus will serve me well in the inevitable future challenges. In the end, the Lord has made me a much better man. I hope that sharing these God stories will help initiate, renew, or expand your personal journey with the Lord through the remainder of your life.

In summary, let me leave you with a beautiful God story. On a business trip in 2019, I flew to Washington, DC, where my daughters, Grace, and Anna, both lived. We met at a quaint Italian restaurant in Georgetown. When I entered the restaurant about ten minutes late, both my daughters locked their eyes upon me; I could see the joy in their faces, which lit up my heart. As we sat down, Anna started to tell me that her and Grace were just talking about what a great dad I was, and how much they appreciated my sacrifices for the family when times were tough. I started to say thank you, but I broke down and could not speak. My daughters then got up from the other side of the table, and they each embraced me as I quietly wept. As I stretched out my arms in a group hug, I immediately realized the reconciliation dream I had multiple times over several years had just materialized, and immense joy overwhelmed me! The hug with my two precious daughters embracing me was one of the happiest moments of my entire life. It took eight long years, but God fulfilled the vision of reconciliation with my daughters that He had put in my dreams, and He did it all in His perfect timing.

The End

CONCLUSION

We live in a complex world built around the ideal called "survival of the fittest." Herbert Spencer coined the phrase in 1869 where he drew parallels between his economic theories with that of Charles Darwin's "natural selection," which is the preservation of favored races in the struggle for life. Self-preservation is quite different for a wealthy individual than it is for someone struggling to make ends meet. The haves get economic security by beating the competition and fighting to be the best in their chosen field. The have-nots are in a battle to put food on the table for themselves and their loved ones.

We live in a world built around self-preservation, economic survival, success, failure, good, evil, fear, greed, love, and hate. However, there is an entirely different world filled with peace, love, security, joy, and wonder. There is an invisible world that exists outside of the physical realm. It's a world of mystery surrounded by the supernatural. It can be discovered by tapping into the spiritual dimension of the universe that is governed by God. As you have just read in this book, a spiritual world filled with supernatural possibilities manifests into reality though the power of intensely directed prayer.

I've experienced many economic highs and lows in the material world. I've been wealthy, but as you have read, I've also lived well below the poverty line. I've experienced some of the best and worst this world has to offer. But in the final analysis, the treasures gained from the spiritual world are what's most valuable to me. These God-given spiritual riches are freely available to you if you will believe in the awesome power of God and His only begotten Son, Jesus Christ.

We are all forced to live by the rules of the material world, and for many of us, the primary focus is building treasures on earth. Those who also live in the spiritual dimension focus much of their attention on building treasures in Heaven. When presented with temporary treasures versus everlasting ones, the choice seems obvious. However, the most important choice to be made is to believe in Jesus Christ or not to believe in Him. This is a huge decision for nonbelievers because the Bible makes it clear as to the consequences of making the wrong choice. The Bible says it's a choice between everlasting life or eternal death. Jesus said: "I am the resurrection and the life. He who believes in Me, though he may die, he shall live." (John 11:25 NKJV).

The decision to choose everlasting life could also mean the difference between life and death here on earth. Let me share a true story. There were two men living in a small town; one looked up when he had financial and legal troubles while the other man looked down. Both men had children of similar ages that went to the same school together. Both men faced substantial financial losses—one in the stock market, and the other in real estate. Both men faced lawsuits, and both faced the prospect of bankruptcy.

The spiritual man understood the supernatural dimension and looked to God for his strength and relief. The worldly man lived by the rules of the material world and put too much of his self-worth around financial status. The result for the worldly man was death as he launched himself off a very steep cliff in what was determined to be a suicide. Faith in God saved the spiritual man while lack of faith killed the worldly man. I share this story because you may be faced with the decision to believe or not to believe in God and His only begotten Son, Jesus Christ. This decision could mean life or death, but according to the Word, it's a firm decision regarding eternal life.

Maybe you're a believer living life with too much emphasis on financial gains in the material world versus spiritual gains in the supernatural world. I was often guilty of this by putting way too much emphasis on financial gains and far too little on spiritual gains. It's totally fine to acquire nice possessions, but as you know, you can't take any of them with you in the end. Therefore, you must pay close attention to your eternal soul that's caged inside your mortal body. Earthly rewards in the material world are temporary while spiritual rewards are everlasting. The true heart you develop on earth will become your spirit in heaven. Your spirit is the invisible but essential part of you that heaven receives when you die.

Maybe you're living life to the fullest, but you wish for much more in your life. It's the *more* that I'm speaking about—more wealth, more success, more approval, more homes, more cars, more sex, and more money. However, the most important part in the "more" is what most people are missing and what they really need. This unmet desire can only be found in the spiritual realm. The missing part, the "more," is a deep and meaningful relationship with God though His Son, Jesus Christ.

The choice is yours to believe or not to believe. You can live solely for this world where everything is temporary, or you can also choose to live in the spiritual dimension, where gifts are everlasting. The spiritual gifts from God are hope, love, faith, joy, peace, confidence, courage, perseverance, and even signs, wonders, visions, and miracles. These are freely available to you right now. Spiritual gifts come from making the firm decision to develop a meaningful and fulfilling relationship with Jesus Christ.

Whether you're making the decision to believe in God or the decision to be a nonbeliever, the choice is yours to make. The wrong choice will fill you with the dissatisfaction of knowing everything you treasure on earth will eventually rust and die, and everyone you love, you will leave behind. The wiser decision will provide you with a life filled with joy from spiritual treasures experienced on earth but built for heaven and eternity. The spiritual treasures of miracles, visions, words of affirmation, answered prayers, and mysterious wonders will be stored inside your heart, mind, and soul. These wonderful spiritual gifts from God will go with you when it's your time to leave this earth.

To help you better understand the parallels between the two worlds, the spiritual and the physical, let me refer to an important Bible story. In Luke 23:42 (KJV), the good thief on the right of the cross said to Jesus: "Lord, remember me when Thou comest into thy kingdom." The believing thief understood Jesus was a King of a spiritual world versus a king of this world. Here's the promise Jesus made to the believing thief near His Cross: "I promise thee, this day thou shalt be with Me in paradise." This promise is the greatest of all gifts available to everyone who believes in Jesus Christ: Paradise.

I'll finish my son's story from the last chapter of this book to further show the parallels between the physical world and the spiritual world. After my son Joe's brutal attack, he pulled me aside to tell me something in private. He was still in a state of shock when he told me his full story: "Dad, when my attacker was on top of me choking me to death, I was outside of my body watching it all take place when I saw a large figure of some kind who appeared to be holding off my attacker. Suddenly, I reappeared in my body where I was face-to-face with my attacker as he screamed repeatedly, "Why won't you just die!" My son pushed his attacker back and nearly bit off the man's finger, which forced his attacker to get up and run away.

My son then asked my opinion of what happened. I told him that I had a strong understanding of what transpired. I explained to my son that I have been praying over his life for an "angel of protection." I told to him that it was only a few nights before his attack when he faced evil, eye-to-eye, that I had prayed for an angel of protection over his life and over the lives of my two daughters. I told Joe that his angel was likely holding the attacker back until he returned into his body so that Joe could be the hero of the story.

During the investigation, the detective discovered a multitude of disturbing things in the attacker's home, filled with various displays of evil. The detective told me the attacker was actually hiding in the house with the intent to rape and kill my daughter Grace. The detective said that if Joe hadn't successfully fought the man off, that I would have had two murdered children. I'm in tears as I type this because I'm so grateful to God for answering my longest held prayer for *angels of protection* over my children.

In the final analysis, it's clear and obvious to me that God wants us to deeply believe in Him and sincerely ask of Him, for us to receive answered prayers and to experience miracles. But in the end, in your final end, the promise of "Paradise" will be the greatest of all gifts you could ever receive. To unbelievers, I pray that you make the wise decision to accept Jesus Christ as your Savior for your journey through life to end in the final destination of all believers: Paradise. To believers, I pray that you make the decision to experience God's supernatural power by claiming His promises with complete faith and true love in your heart for Him and His Son—Jesus Christ.

In summary, I decided to do a final random Bible opening for you by asking the Lord what words He wanted me to share with you. He took me directly to Luke 6:20–23 (AMP):

> And solemnly lifting up His eyes on His disciples, He said: Blessed are you poor and lowly and afflicted, for the kingdom of God is yours!

> Blessed are you who hunger and seek with eager desire now, for you shall be filled and completely satisfied! Blessed are you who weep and sob now, for you shall laugh!

> Blessed are you when people despise you, and when they exclude and excommunicate you and revile and denounce you and defame and cast out and spurn your name as evil on account of the Son of Man.

> Rejoice and be glad at such a time and exult and leap for joy, for behold, your reward is rich and great and strong and intense and abundant in heaven; for even so their forefathers treated the prophets.

EPILOGUE

One evening, I woke in the middle of the night with a deep sense of dread. I was under attack by the enemy shooting arrows of sorrow and despair into my heart. In response to my feeling of dread, I prayed extensively with my arms outstretched. I asked Jesus to speak directly to me and specifically to me as I was feeling very discouraged. I asked to hear His voice and His exact words of encouragement to me. In desperation, I begged Jesus to please let me know that everything that happened to me was truly from Him.

Lo and behold, the very next morning, I get a message in my message inbox from a guy named Gary who said: "I have a word directly from the Lord for you." Gary was from the online trading community where I was a contributor. Even though I never met this man, I sent him my personal email address as he requested. I did not include a couple of sentences that were for my eyes only, but this is what Gary emailed me:

Ron, I pick up pen and write—I put the pen down. The Lord's words to you:

> Ron, the fire of everlasting justice and the complete everlasting truth, greet you and love you for you have sought My face in truth and calmed storms in men's hearts.

> I have broken the back of sin at the cross and washed all who would be washed.

The dam of My love has burst over the whole of My creation, and what has been bought back at great price is secure.

I have a fire of My love in reservation for you Ron, a flame of understanding that will cut through dimensional boundaries and observe what cannot be seen with the naked eye.

You, My son, will pick up a rod of truth and not be ashamed to explain what it is that you carry.

Ron, the storms on the horizon are the signs of the times.

The world is on a great diet to see how much of Me they can lose. The world needs to bulk up in Me and put the strength of My Spirit to the test and prove My word faithful.

Ron, I have given to you great insight, and now I, your Lord, place a demand on you to speak where you have previously feared to tread.

Do not favor men who wade in darkness because they navigate the world system well. Glean what you must but place your heart with those who keep what I have kept.

Do not be troubled that you have not broken through to what you consider the next level, for I am the ultimate arbiter when accounts are settled. Ron, stay long your Savior for I have much more in reserve to issue you.

Ron, I want you to remember that I walked among the elites and was mocked by the same. Do not apologize for Me or for what you know to be true. Have you known Satan to ever be apologetic or timid?

Great is your faithfulness for you have not forgotten to be thankful. Ron, you are My illumination in a darkening generation.

The triumph of My light is the celebration after a great victory that has bought back all that have been sold short by sin.

I am victory, Ron.

I am the everlasting covenant.

I am the high tower of the man that would receive Me into his heart by way of a heart's simple confession.

I am a refuge, Ron.

I want the torch of My love to operate in tandem with signs following great rivers of My manifest presence that would break hard hearts.

Ron, I preached Myself with My hands before I spoke to the heart with My mouth. Dear one, it is many times that the signs of the anointed man will open the heart that has been locked.

The King of Glory, Ron, your Lord strong and mighty loves you and has you kept.

Deposit the endless supply of who I am, for My great love is placing a demand on you. Stand and be counted in a generation that would have you sit and be silent.

Make a funnel with your hands and I will fill you that when you are hard pressed it will be I that speaks for you.

Ron, I want you to be My fire that is feared in the heavenly realm and takes ground from the enemy for the lost are found and strongholds are eliminated.

Let the banner of your Master fly unfurled in the wind of His Spirit, being both bold and wise. Be mindful always of the devil's landmines and his destructive devices.

The devil used the device of the tongue to slander Me where I walked, so do not expect rose petals to walk on, thrown by a world that wants to shut Me up.

Ron, I have tested your mettle and now I would turn up the volume of your service. The fire of My service is the great illumination of a servant who has seen the end from the beginning, for the light of who I am is a lamp to his feet and a light to his path.

Ron, you are the subject of My great love, and I will never ever leave or forsake you. Do not fear.

As you can imagine, the impeccable timing of this email filled with such powerful words sent me into a state of spiritual bewilderment! I had never spoken to Gary on the phone or met him in person, but it was time for us to speak after receiving such a perfectly timed email. We were on the phone for hours. He confirmed to me that the time he received these words from the Lord was about the time I was praying to Jesus to hear His voice and His exact words to me.

In summary, if Gary had sent this email to me any other time than the morning after my specific and unique prayer request to Jesus, I would have had doubts about its legitimacy. However, the fact that Gary sent that email to me the very next day after my intense night of prayer, I believe Jesus answered me through one of His modern-day prophets. It's incredible to think the good Lord spoke these specific words to me, but it appears that He did. Once again, Jesus powerfully answered yet another one of my distress prayers. My prayer to end this book: *Thank You, Jesus, for Your blessings and for confirming all the miraculous events that happened during the writing of this book. And Lord, thank You for using me as Your instrument to write this book in order to empower others to seek You and to find You and to believe in Your power to answer their prayers and to create miracles in their lives. Amen.*

Lightning Source UK Ltd.
Milton Keynes UK
UKHW012022020921
389944UK00007B/456/J